Richard Gerver

change

Learn to Love It,
Learn to Lead It

PORTFOLIO
PENGUIN

PORTFOLIO PENGUIN

Published by the Penguin Group

Penguin Books Ltd, 80 Strand, London WC2R ORL, England

Penguin Group (USA) Inc., 375 Hudson Street, New York, New York 10014, USA

Penguin Group (Canada), 90 Eglinton Avenue East, Suite 700, Toronto, Ontario,
Canada M4P 2Y3 (a division of Pearson Penguin Canada Inc.)

Penguin Ireland, 25 St Stephen's Green, Dublin 2, Ireland
(a division of Penguin Books Ltd)

Penguin Group (Australia), 707 Collins Street, Melbourne,
Victoria 3008, Australia (a division of Pearson Australia Group Pty Ltd)

Penguin Books India Pvt Ltd, 11 Community Centre,
Panchsheel Park, New Delhi – 110 017, India

Penguin Group (NZ), 67 Apollo Drive, Rosedale, Auckland 0632,
New Zealand (a division of Pearson New Zealand Ltd)

Penguin Books (South Africa) (Pty) Ltd, Block D, Rosebank Office Park,
181 Jan Smuts Avenue, Parktown North, Gauteng 2193, South Africa

Penguin Books Ltd, Registered Offices: 80 Strand, London WC2R ORL, England

www.penguin.com

First published 2013
003

Set in Quadraat
Typeset by Richard Marston
Printed in China

ISBN: 978–0–670–92234–5

To David Drew Smythe, for helping me to change the way I see the world

R.I.P.

# CONTENTS

# PROLOGUE

When I was five years old my father took me to the East End of London to show me where he worked. It was an old, beaten-up warehouse on the edge of a Thameside wharf, filled with wood of all types from all over the world, destined for the furniture industry.

I remember being overawed by the smell of the timber and fascinated by an ancient telephone exchange full of wires and copper connectors. There were piles of important papers scattered over my father's imposing desk and a photograph of my great-grandfather on the wall opposite. This had been his business, handed down to his son and grandson, a business built by an immigrant with a dream, by a man who had escaped a war-torn Europe.

He arrived on these shores with nothing but the clothes on his back and the family he cherished, and stood on this spot looking beyond the clouds of death and misery, right up into the sky, to the moon and stars beyond, believing that there was a future, that he would see the sun rise in better, safer times. But he would have known that it was up to him to master the uncertainty, the changes and the challenges that faced him.

Forty years later I was in a stadium constructed within shouting distance of that same warehouse. On the night of 29 August 2012, Professor Stephen Hawking addressed the opening ceremony of the 2012 London Paralympic Games with these words: 'Look up at the stars and not down at your feet. Try to make sense of what you see, and wonder about what makes the universe exist. Be curious.'

Professor Hawking celebrated the power of the human spirit and our extraordinary capacity to evolve, change and challenge adversity.

Listening to those words was Martine Wright, the sitting volleyball star whose journey began on 6 July 2005 when she went out with friends from work to celebrate the awarding of the Olympics and Paralympics to London. A slight hangover meant that the next morning she found herself sitting next to a suicide bomber on a later tube train than she would have usually taken. Split seconds are all that it takes to change the course of our lives. The explosion ripped through the train carriage and her lower body. As part of her recovery she started playing sitting volleyball and was now representing Team GB as an elite athlete, competing, not watching as the spectator she might originally have expected to be.

As the flame was lit and those beautiful stems drew up to form the symbol of the Games, 80,000 people and their stories came together with the billions watching at home, a moment of convergence connected by the only real constant: change.

Martine Wright and Stephen Hawking are both inspirational. Their stories have led others to new ways of thinking, behaving and living. They have mastered change and uncertainty in the most extreme of circumstances, and have been labelled rightly by broadcasters and journalists as superhuman.

The truth, though, is that change is a part of our lives. In this book I am going to give my personal take on how we can all thrive in the ever-shifting era we live in, times that are fast-moving and difficult to control. I will explore how we can move forward and take charge, personally and professionally. How we can rediscover a love of change. How we can learn to embrace change, lead it and pass on its legacy.

# EXPLORE

'We are born learners. We arrive in
this world with inquiring minds.'

# Change

I was painfully shy and nervy as a young boy, and at school I had a couple of early, disastrous run-ins with drama and performing. One year I was given the privilege of singing the first verse of 'Once in Royal David's City' as a solo to introduce the Christmas carol service. I opened my mouth when the big moment arrived. My throat dried. Nothing emerged other than a strangulated squawk. Everyone there shared in my embarrassment and humiliation.

Strangely, despite the trauma of that moment, I fell in love with the idea of performing, of being someone else, of having the freedom to escape from my own clumsy persona. I had a great teacher who stuck by me and encouraged me. He helped me bounce back from any setbacks. I was given better and better roles. The slight stutter I occasionally experienced vanished. My confidence blossomed. The experience of performance was all about overcoming fears and realizing that I could do it, that I could change myself.

You have probably experienced a similar moment, when fear threatens to block your progress. Fear of change is so often the result of imagined consequences rather than reality. I want to show you how you can embrace change and free yourself to make significant leaps forward.

The trick is to go right back to the beginning.

As babies we are delivered into a world of constant change, into a place that is entirely strange and unknown to us. We start out with no awareness of the skills we will need to make sense of the space and time we inhabit, yet we all grow up and, remarkably, very few of us go mad or have

Explore

*Fear of change is so often the result of imagined consequences rather than reality.*

a breakdown during that tumultuous time. In fact we learn and adapt more in those early years than we do in the rest of our days. We learn to walk, to talk, to understand body language and interpret the subtleties of facial and vocal intonation, all out of nothing.

So why, as we grow up, do we lose this instinctive ability to embrace and deal with change?

I spent many years in education, as both a teacher and head teacher. I realized that the notion that people need to be taught how to learn is ridiculous, because we are born learners. We arrive in this world with inquiring minds. We have learned a vast amount before we go to school. The speed at which we learn as infants is truly inspirational.

Then educators interfere with the natural process by putting these highly talented, extraordinary, adaptable learning machines – or children, as we

Change

prefer to call them – into an environment where we teach them to be controlled.

Somewhere during the process of growing up, going through education and then heading into work, change ceases to be internal and intrinsic and becomes an external force, or at least that is how we perceive it. Change, we think, is something that only happens when we are told to change, forced to change – when we lose a job, perhaps – or when we are presented by our bosses with a 'change strategy'.

*Our personal response to change is affected by those turning points when we have undergone significant changes in our own lives.*

We never stop changing, but how we react to it determines whether we feel good or bad about it. We tend to be comfortable with change if we believe we are in control of it, and if we think it's for our own good. But we resent change, and resent it strongly, if we think it is not going to benefit us, that we have not chosen to be involved in it or that we have no control over it.

Explore

A starting point for analysing our personal response to change is to understand that it grows directly out of our own experiences, and is affected by those turning points when we have undergone significant changes in our own lives.

## MY JOURNEY

I was born into a middle-class, north-London family, a Jewish family – which is significant because in the 1960s we were still in an era when my grandparents were relatively recent immigrants. Their vision of the future involved the family becoming part of British society, and their children enjoying a first-rate education and then going into the professions. My father worked in his family's timber business, and was doing well; my mother's family had also been successful. So they sent me off on their preferred route, to a private school.

I loved my early school days, because I was allowed to be creative and free, and that suited me since I wasn't what was thought of as a typical

Change

boy: I enjoyed writing, drama, the arts. That was fine until I was thirteen, at which point I was dispatched to Mill Hill, a school where sport, rugby in particular, was very important. Suddenly I didn't fit in. I was neither strongly academic nor especially good at sport, and I certainly had no talent for rugby (although I loved watching it). The way I reacted to this change was to become a bit of an agitator, to try and shake things up.

This was, however, at a time when conventional wisdom decreed I should have been craving security and continuity following my parents' divorce when I was ten. It is of great credit to my mother, with whom I stayed after the divorce, and my grandparents, that I found myself being quite challenging in school, not so much by exhibiting the disruptive behaviour characteristic of many children in such circumstances, but more cerebrally in thinking: *Why should this be convention, why do we always have to do things this way?*

In my first year at Mill Hill I discovered that

the older kids were essentially running the place. If you turned up with any interesting new sweets or snacks, they had first dibs on whatever you brought in. Aged thirteen, I marched into my housemaster's office and demanded to know why that had to be the case. 'Because,' he said, 'you'll go through it, and you'll earn your stripes, and when you're older, you'll do the same.' 'Well, that's ridiculous,' I said. 'I think it's morally wrong, so I don't want to do that.' I was not prepared to accept the status quo.

In the same way, when I wrote essays I would often go against everything my teacher had asked me to write about, because I objected to being told what to think. There was an element of wanting to kick against the system – not unusual at that age, of course – but by the time I got to A levels, my resentment had grown extremely strong. I left school at eighteen having no desire to go anywhere near education ever again – an irony, given my later career.

All I wanted to do at the time was to be an actor, but I scorned convention, did not apply for any

Change

college courses and decided I was going to build an acting career with absolutely no training. Everyone around me was convinced I was mad; everyone, that is, other than my mum, who told me I should listen to my heart, follow my dream. It must have been a courageous thing for her to do, to sit back and watch me make all the mistakes and follow paths that led nowhere. I am sure at times she was terrified about where I'd end up – I was making some really bad choices – but of course it was an incredibly powerful learning experience.

After a couple of years of trying and failing at acting, and realizing that although I was a competent school actor I was not good enough to make a career out of it, I decided, finally, to go to college. I found a course at Derby College of Higher Education, the last place anyone from a posh school like Mill Hill would ever go, which was one of the first colleges to offer a modular degree in what was called 'Writing For Publication, Visual Communication and Performance' – and I loved it.

And then everything did change, because in my first year at Derby I met a young woman, Lynne, who was in her final year of training to be a teacher. She got herself a teaching job in Derby, so we carried on seeing each other. One day, just as I was about to go into my second year, she asked me, 'Richard, on your days off would you come in and do some drama with my kids? They would love it, and I hate drama.' Of course I would.

It sounds really daft, but it's true: I fell in love with both her and teaching at the same time, and ended up wedded to both. And my priorities shifted. I suddenly found a world where I belonged. It was all the things I was good at: performance and communication. So at that moment of change, when I decided to follow a career in education, I was passionate about it. I knew what the alternatives were and I had become much more focused.

I realize now that I was open to the possibility of change and interested in the potential it offered. The received wisdom from many of those who were older and ostensibly wiser was always to look for

Change

the safe option, and when you had it, to stick, like playing blackjack. But there was always another side in me that said, and still says, 'I love adventure, meeting new people, seeing new things, going to new places. Hit me!'

Explore

# Challenge for Change #1

What do you do at the 'sat nav moment'? We have all grown used to allowing the sat nav to tell us how to drive from A to B, trusting the judgement calls it makes. When you reach a crossroads, do you always think, *I'll just go straight on because that's where the sat nav is telling me to go* – or are you prepared to wonder what might happen if you took the left or right turning? Are you willing to ask, *Where else could I go now?* Or does the very idea make you feel unsettled? Are you afraid of change?

At eighteen, I felt able to branch away from the path everyone expected me to take because I knew my mother and grandparents would always be supportive. The way they had brought me up, the way they talked to me, the way they interacted

Change

with me, always encouraged me to go out and have adventures, with the reassurance that everything would be all right because they were there for me. It was like being giving permission to go off and walk in space, since there was a tether attached.

Put simply, I knew where home was. And that is important because there is no doubt that stability is an essential part of anyone's spirit of adventure. To go back to the sat nav analogy, you can go for a drive on a Sunday afternoon, keep exploring and end up in the middle of bloody nowhere, but you can always press HOME on the sat nav.

## THE 'BUSYNESS' TRAP

Change does not have to be unsettling. It is not about ripping up your roots and throwing everything else that went before out of the window.

In recent times the freedom to explore, knowing there is a safe return, has dwindled, has become constrained. Society no longer wants our kids to bunk over the garden fence and be free to roam the

Explore

woods all day. And in part the educational system itself does that to us. We are taught that there are fixed routes; boundaries that must not be crossed.

In the Victorian era mass education and mass industrialism were being refined at the same time, and society wanted an education system that would prepare a workforce for the industrial age. It was all about locking down certainty, creating efficiency, telling people, 'We are going to map out everything for you in advance, so that when you find work in a factory or an office you will know exactly when and how to clock in, what your duties will be, how to carry them out efficiently, how to clock out at night.'

'Time and motion' – a phrase that was central to the workplace in the mid-twentieth century – was introduced through the studies of Frank and Lillian Gilbreth in the 1920s, based on the work of Frederick Winslow Taylor, an American mechanical engineer who explored the science of productivity and efficiency in the workplace. His 1911 monograph, *The Principles of Scientific*

Change

*Management*, became the rule book – and as a consequence 'Taylorism' the byword – by which business and industry drove forward; efficiency was the Holy Grail of the industrial age. It was the only way to remain competitive as new nations became industrialized and competed in an increasingly global market.

Those principles were phenomenally successful and were perfected by the industrial powerhouses of the Asian continent – Japan and China – but they counted on product and service remaining the same. They are principles based on efficiency not evolution.

*Our businesses turned into silos, employees became cogs in machines.*

I am neither an economist nor an industrialist but it strikes me that these principles, so effective in their way and appropriate for their time, were adopted at a great cost – a sacrifice for which many are now paying dear. Our businesses turned into silos, bunkered organizations in which employees became cogs in machines, white collar or blue collar. We got

Explore

our heads down. Ultimately, that approach became fixed, entrenched, inflexible, a rigidity of thinking, putting down roots to which education is still firmly anchored.

From an early age we were all taught to aspire to having a mortgage, a dog, 2.4 kids. The education system was, and still is, primarily concerned with proving to us that we are efficient: learn it, remember it, demonstrate it. Such a robotic approach worked for previous generations, particularly after the uncertainty of two world wars, following which there was a desire to return to security and solidity. The problem is we still have the same system more than fifty years on: parents and grandparents of young people possess that same mindset, as do managers in the majority of companies.

For the most part, people want to live happy and rewarding lives; they work hard and do their best for their families, friends and workplaces. However, the trap described as 'busyness' by Andy Cope in his book *The Art of Being Brilliant* is a significant factor in the reason for the current ignorance of the value

Change

of change. People are leading increasingly frenetic, complex lives, and companies are functioning under more and more challenging conditions, but seem to be hampered by the principles that drove increased productivity in the twentieth century.

What happened to the instinctive sense of awe and wonder we possessed as children?

I have spent many years challenging my colleagues in education to find out just why we lose that magic, the ability to keep exploring, challenging and changing, and why so many of us begin to melt into the crowd.

Childhood becomes a high-risk emotional game; we spend most of our daily lives in school, where we experience a world in which we must get things right; we are judged by how many questions we get correct, how well we score in our tests and how often we put our hands up and give the teacher the desired response. Consequently, for much of the time, we associate work (an extension of school) with a lack of empowerment and heightened risk, treating it as a prolonged assessment.

Explore

*So many people who worry about change and the unknown are often just scared: scared of exposing their weaknesses, their lack of confidence and their insecurities.*

The growing pressures on growing children make them feel less secure and less treasured. Survival changes from an implicit instinct to an explicit strategy, and then we reach adulthood and the raft of challenges that brings. In the workplace, how secure and treasured do many of us feel?

Change feels frightening. So many people who worry about change and the unknown are often just scared: scared of exposing their weaknesses, their lack of confidence and their insecurities. I call them 'wasp swallowers', those people we all know who always follow a comment or feedback with a 'But . . .' They lack the strength to confront the challenges they face.

Often the most aggressive bullies on the school playground are the least confident pupils, and usually those most resistant to change. When dealing with them, the important thing is to find a point of connection, to discern the lack of confidence behind the bravado and begin to build context and capacity – just as my drama teacher at school did with me, helping me conquer my anxieties by skilfully guiding me to overcome small but significant barriers.

## 20 PER CENT TIME

Many organizations, when planning their staff development, become obsessed about the systematic, outward results from specific job roles. They forget about personal development and the importance of emotive connections. Not surprisingly people become automatons, with a soulless attitude to their work and professional development.

The best staff development takes into account potential, not just delivery. Google gives each employee what they call '20 per cent time', a fifth

Explore

of the working week set aside for su⌐
development. The expectation is t'
use that time for working up nev
ing personal research, career dev⌐
whatever they do is owned and
activated by the individual and not
imposed by a line manager.

There are huge lessons here for
the individual. We live in a society
obsessed with 'pigeon-holing'.
From an early age we are given labels which can so
easily define our lives. At school, we are herded into
tribes, academic and social. Often we find ourselves
stuck in the wrong one, which can have a damaging
impact on our potential and well-being.

This is an issue explored brilliantly by Sir Ken
Robinson in his book *The Element*. He raises the
notion of a tribe as having two distinct ideas:
domains – which he defines as the activities and
disciplines that people are engaged in, such as
acting, music, physics, sports – and fields, which
refers to the other people engaged in it.

*From⌐
we are given ⌐
which can so easily
define our lives.*

Change

he problem for many is that we are expected to function in certain domains with a field of people who, it is assumed, are like-minded because it is the domain they too are told to inhabit. Once placed in a domain it is very hard to break out, and the field becomes the one that you are socialized to accept.

I have a friend I have known since we were three. On the surface we had little in common. He was perfect: clever, brilliant at sports, good-looking and highly likeable. He had everything. When we were older and went on holidays together, girls would want to meet me, but only so that it would get them closer to him. At school, he was pushed to hang with the sporty crowd; he was the rugby player, the man's man. Underneath, however, he was highly artistic, creative, a deeply sensitive boy.

When he left school he was a little bit of a mess, emotionally not really sure what he was, what he wanted to be, or whether he really belonged in the crowd he was expected to be part of. As

Explore

a result, he spent a couple of years travelling, in order to escape and have time to reassess. By the time he returned home he had realized that the life projected on to him was only going to make him unhappy. He started making jewellery and art, became fascinated by photography and visual forms of communication. Now he leads an eclectic life far away from the young man he was, and far happier than he had felt living life in his pigeon hole. It has left him scarred, however, and if I am honest I am not sure that he has ever reached his true potential. I have always found it sad that he needed to escape the influences in his life in order to begin to find out who he really was, and to see the lasting damage that being pushed into the wrong tribe has had on him.

By contrast I am fascinated by the stories of some of our most successful entrepreneurs – Duncan Bannatyne, Alan Sugar or Michelle Mone, for example. So many of them describe their journeys as tough: difficult childhoods, poor academic performance, early business failures.

Change

But they are undeniably achievers. They all say that the great entrepreneurs fail and fail again, but never give up, and always learn.

What that suggests to me is that they are not waiting for someone else to come along and provide the answers, to make everything all right with the wave of a magic wand. They realized the course of their lives would be created by their own decisions and actions. They made change happen.

In fast-changing times it is time to take control ourselves once again. It is time for us to rediscover the thrill of change.

Explore

# Explore

- Learn to question your responses to new, unexpected or unwelcome events and circumstances. Ask yourself why you react in the way you do. Being objective and reflective are crucial skills to develop if you are to master change.

- Spend time really exploring what unsettles you – nothing too dramatic: you don't need to go and lie in a bed of spiders if that is what frightens you most. Force yourself to overcome one small fear every week.

- If, for example, you find the idea of going to the cinema by yourself unsettling, pick a film, buy a ticket, chew some popcorn and then go home knowing you have dealt with that fear. Most fears are irrational and based on perception rather than reality. You will only believe that when you have overcome a few.

Change

- You can share the challenge with someone you trust so that they are there to encourage, support and guide you.

- If you manage people, mentor them to do the same as often as is practical and viable.

- Remind yourself what it was like to be a very young child, when every moment was new, fresh and uncontrolled. This will reconnect you with the innate confidence we have at that age to experience change, understand it, lock it in and move on. Imagine how much more productive we would be if we could start to think a little more like four-year-olds again.

Explore

Change

# REFRESH

'The twenty-first century is the era
when the pace of change has finally
overtaken our ability to control it.
And we are finding this unbelievably
difficult to come to terms with.'

# Change

I was first introduced to the internet in the early
1990s. A friend who was also a teacher invited me
over to his house to look at this 'online' thing.
He had his computer wired up to a box plugged
into his phone line; it took ages to boot up. After
much humming, buzzing and screeching I saw my
first-ever web page.

'Look,' my friend said with tangible excitement.
'You can get access to the White House web page.'
I was impressed, briefly, but once I had got over the
idea that I could see Bill Clinton's public diary, my
reaction to the technology was that it was expensive

and clunky. By the time I had driven home I had come to the conclusion that it was a good talking point but a bit of a gimmick. Within a couple of years, of course, I didn't just want my own internet access, I *needed* it. Less than twenty years later, like everyone else, I cannot imagine life without it. That has been change in palpable, real-time, culture-altering action.

People and organizations are forced to confront change all the time: changes in personal circumstances, health, wealth, job security. In all cases there are weights in favour or against that lift and fall. There are complex struggles with emotions of self-esteem, confidence, resilience, belief, logic, fantasy and fear.

The world has become an uncertain, unstable and exponentially changing place. A feeling of powerlessness has become the most brutal disease of the twenty-first century. There is a growing sense of anger and resentment, of disconnection and disenfranchisement, that is showing itself, in its extremes, through increased levels of violence on

Refresh

the streets of Britain. Many people feel that they no longer have much choice; many feel that the locus of control has never been so far out of reach. We are looking for help, support, guidance or just a reassuring hand.

Change is exciting, and it always has been. It is human nature to explore, to question, to bungee jump, even to free fall from the edge of space, but it seems to be something so few embrace and which, worryingly, is diminishing among the majority. As the stakes are raised only the high-rolling gamblers remain. Most people will tell you that gambling is irresponsible; yet of those who do gamble, the majority wager only what they can afford to lose. It is only a very few who just keep rolling the dice. Too often people equate any form of change with recklessness and unnecessary risk.

*Too often people equate any form of change with recklessness and unnecessary risk.*

So it is that change has become for many an unnatural and, at best, uncomfortable concept.

Change

*At what point did we start to wish that
Christmas was just like it used to be,
for television programmes that crackled
in black and white?*

That is why, when things are uncertain or appear
to be beyond our control, our instinct is to curl up
with some sentimental songs, a box of chocolates
and a cuddly jumper. It is a natural reaction, born
out of the instinct to be nurtured and protected.
It is a cycle. The more dangerous and uncertain the
world appears to be, the more intensive our primal
urge to keep ourselves and our loved ones safe.

Often, we retreat into nostalgia. For me it begins
as summer turns to autumn, when the dark nights
creep in and the leaves start to cascade from the
trees. It is then that I, like the winter-shy wildlife,
prepare to hunker down. My mindset shifts away
from the expansive freedom and endless days
of summer. As the chill hits the air, I feel the
urge to build a fire and huddle in a stretched and

Refresh

threadbare sweater, right there in the living room. Occasionally, as a special treat, I'll even light one of those scented candles that smell, like my mother's kitchen, of cookies, cinnamon, caramel or winter spice.

When did we first become nostalgic? At what point did we start to wish that Christmas was just like it used to be, for television programmes that crackled in black and white? There is no doubt that nostalgia brings a certain peace and warmth, a protective glow.

Scientific research into nostalgia is limited, but Tim Wildschut and his team from Southampton University have underlined what many instinctively believe. In a 2006 report for the *Journal of Personality and Social Psychology* he states that the brain is an incredibly energy-intensive organ, on average using more glucose than our muscles every day. So it goes without saying that the brain does not usually do anything without a very good reason. Why, then, is nostalgia important? Wildschut found that with a brain that supports consciousness come problems

Change

born from self-awareness. The neuroscience involved is an issue too tangled to unpick here, but we have all experienced the problems that come with it: depression, self-doubt and lack of motivation.

I enjoy the feeling of nostalgia, but I don't dwell on it when the sun is shining and I am riding on the crest of a wave. I don't hanker for the past when I'm living in the moment, on stage giving a speech, playing sport (badly) or challenging colleagues or friends in tense debate.

My first real memory of constructing a nostalgic act was when I was thirteen and had gone through a particularly messy break-up with my 'long-term' girlfriend of two weeks. Our special song had been 'Tears in Heaven' by Eric Clapton, and the day she dumped me I retreated to my bedroom and played it endlessly, reliving our first dance, the first kiss, over and over again. It is no accident that, as times become more uncertain and susceptible to change, so our desire grows for the past, for a time of familiarity and security. Since the dawn of the

Refresh

new millennium nostalgia has become a lifestyle product, with bands re-forming after thirty years, reruns and remakes of classic films and television programmes and, most telling perhaps, the rise in advertising campaigns that deliberately tap into the warmth of our past.

It appeals because the world is going through a period of uncertainty: the financial crisis, threats to the environment, socio-ethnic strife, globalization. Our instinct – just like our parents' and grandparents' instinct in times of crisis – is to lock back into certainty. So we hear companies and people talking about 'hunkering down', 'riding the financial storm', 'waiting for it to pass'.

Because the future has become so uncertain on so many levels, we have to move away from an

*We have to move away from an industrial mindset, one obsessed with targets, productivity and conformity, to one that is far more organic in nature.*

Change

industrial mindset, one obsessed with targets, productivity and conformity, to one that is far more organic in nature. We need to be able to move beyond coping with change as something that only happens every few years. Change is no longer an option, or something you can review periodically; it has gone from being an oscillating wave to a full-blown tsunami that threatens to sweep away so many before it.

## NEW TARGETS

These new truths seem almost counter-intuitive to many of us, given our educational and social upbringing. I remember when performance management systems were introduced into the British education system during the mid-1990s and we were all trained in the art of target-setting. The mantra was to devise and implement SMART targets.

Refresh

S – SPECIFIC: the target must say exactly what needs to be learned or done.

M – MEASURABLE: it must say exactly how this can be measured.

A – ACHIEVABLE: the target must not be too hard or too large; better to have several small targets leading to a larger goal.

R – REALISTIC: it must be possible to get access to any training, books or help needed to meet the target.

T – TIMED: there should be set time limits for achieving the target.

I am not dismissing this approach, as it provided a clear structure for professional expectations and a teaching methodology that was highly focused on outcomes. It created the kind of rigorous approach that was lacking in some schools. SMART can be a powerful tool, as indeed it has been for many years

Change

in the industrial sector. But it is now a flawed tool for the organic age we live in.

SMART targets work when you are heading for fixed outputs, but limit the potential for transformation or even the evolution of practice. Most athletes are used to working with SMART targets: runners, for example, know the distance of their race and the fixed number of variables that can be developed to improve performance. How well those variables are developed can make the difference between success and failure at the very highest level. But that isn't the whole story.

Dave Brailsford, who oversaw the transformation of the Great Britain track cycling team as well as Bradley Wiggins's 2012 Tour de France triumph, made a huge number of changes to cycling's rituals. He ended the culture of repetitive, intense training. He broke down every component part of cycling and asked questions of aspects never before explored in that sport: deep psychology, the alloys in the equipment, the colour of the kit, the use of music and multi-disciplinary training.

Refresh

He proved that to be world beaters you must move beyond SMART and not rely on such targets to maximize potential. The targets should be used as a tool within a system – but the system itself must encompass more.

## Challenge for Change #2

We need to build change into the very fabric of our organizations and cultures. We must learn to recognize that the ability to change is built on the ability to question, to challenge and to live outside a comfort zone.

The wisest among us know that change is – and always has been – unavoidable. Even as a lifelong Arsenal fan I look in admiration at the ability of Sir Alex Ferguson to incorporate an appreciation of change into the culture at Manchester United.

Change

Since 1986, when Ferguson was first appointed manager at Old Trafford, he has maintained a policy of freshening up his coaching staff by using numerous assistant managers. This has been a deliberate strategy, as he realized that the game of football would constantly evolve through new tactical systems, coaching techniques and training regimes. Shifts in power would change depending on who could adopt and adapt most successfully.

Since Alex Ferguson had no intention of leaving Manchester United and was determined to build a legacy that would turn them into one of the most successful clubs in football history, he was ready to bring in people who would challenge his own thinking. And how well it has worked. At Arsenal, in comparison, Arsène Wenger has retained essentially the same team of coaches and assistants around him, changing nothing about his systems and structures, believing in continuity. After a few years of extraordinary success – driven by Wenger's vision and what at the time were progressive methods – the club's fortunes have stagnated.

Refresh

The twenty-first century is a seminal period. In the past most people could keep up with change; now, though, many are dropping by the wayside, unable to keep pace. For most of the twentieth century change could be largely avoided as long as productivity was unaffected. Individuals could own a home, tie down a job for life having perfected a skill or a bank of professional knowledge; people understood the system and learned to play it. Organizations knew their roles, they understood their markets, their services, their products and they worked on efficiencies and systems to deliver them with precision and continuity.

But certainty is no longer within our control. The ongoing economic crisis has disguised the real issue. I think we have reached a tipping point where technological advancement has led to such a rapid continuum of change that we are powerless to direct its course. We are living in the first age when we no longer determine the rate of change. My concern is that unless we accept this, and transform the way we think, behave, manage and prepare the

Change

next generation, we are going to find it harder and harder to keep up.

Often the 'fight or flight' response we experience when we are threatened puts us into a state of denial, and this is what I believe is happening en masse. We can see the problems, but think it's someone else's job to solve them.

We have a tendency to set targets temporally. By date x I will achieve y. For many teachers, the school year is the length of the journey, for those in the corporate world it is often marked by the end of the financial calendar. Sadly, for many the annual target is survival: personal and professional. People see the targets and routines in their working lives as hurdles that need to be jumped without falling as they strive for the finish line. We are not born that way, though; we are born always looking for the adventure to come, we meet each challenge because it is there, not because

*People see the targets and routines in their working lives as hurdles that need to be jumped without falling as they strive for the finish line.*

Refresh

it leads us to an end point, and we have no concept of a finish line.

This state of affairs is largely of our own making, as team members await the next great edict from above. Many of us only want to know what is expected of us, by when and how we will be evaluated. It is interesting to see people's reaction to change strategies; most want to know what it will look like and how long it will take so that they can psychologically prepare themselves for a fixed journey and participate accordingly. The danger of this kind of approach, of course, is its limitation on potential development and growth: if Sir James Dyson had stuck to constructing Airfix plastic models, step by step, never deviating from the instructions, we might never have ended up with his reinvention of the vacuum cleaner.

A great many of us are conditioned to think and behave by the previous generation, who naturally had the same guidance from the generation before them, and so it went. While for the most part this is a binding factor in society, the simple fact is that

Change

as the world turns and we as a species continue to evolve at an extraordinary rate, the attitudes that kept our parents safe and secure will not necessarily help us or our children.

The words we use as adults and the words we hear when we are young have a profound impact on our developing psyche. How often have you caught yourself saying to your own children the same words you heard from your own parents: 'Don't do that, you might . . .' or 'Did you get it right? Oh, well done!'

A career in teaching was tailor made for the child I was. As a boy I loved timetables and schedules. I would always want to know what we were doing, at what time, where and when, for weeks in advance. Becoming a teacher seemed the obvious choice: timetables, bells and an ordered existence.

Our schooldays shape what we become, and the system itself is not designed to prepare us to live with change and uncertainty. Quite the opposite. Days are highly structured and ordered; we are

Refresh

trained to function in a framework of regime and familiarity.

Often I address groups of people about change and the imperative for fundamental transformation. In the session we will reach a consensus, a definite agreement that radical action is needed. But then, as we really start to explore the necessary action, people drift away. I saw this for the first time when I worked for a company selling the very earliest iteration of cellular phones: handsets with a power supply the size of a car battery.

At the time, 'mobile' phones would sell for four-figure sums and the cost of calls was frightening. I worked for a firm whose founder, a young entrepreneur, had seen the potential early, created the business with a loan from his parents and made a small fortune for himself inside three years by selling the equipment at a sizeable mark-up.

One day he walked into the office for a meeting with his board of directors and told them that he wanted to slash the cost of the phones and sell them at virtually cost price. He knew change

Change

was sweeping the industry and that the airtime providers were only interested in the profits from call charges. The directors thought he was mad and offered to buy him out; which they did, for millions. The new owners continued to plough the furrow of high-cost units and within two years of the takeover had gone bust. It was not that the directors had failed to see the founder's point but they felt it was too big a risk to change the business model they knew.

## GAME CHANGE

In the current climate organizations are shedding jobs, restructuring. The explanation is that it is a result of the economic crisis. But the world has changed anyway and therefore the goalposts for many businesses have shifted irrevocably. Individuals blame the organization for the fact that they are now unemployed, the organizations blame the unemployment on the restructuring, and no one has stopped to wonder whether this is

Refresh

the beginning of a seismic shift in the commercial landscape.

This is something we need to take control of in a different way. It is all about people now, not about systems.

Yet everyone is still scrabbling around looking for the new structure. I was recently leading a session at a well-known financial services company; it became clear that my audience believed that if only they could learn to find the new system, the new algorithm that would enable them to control their world again, they would be able to revert to the default setting. The reality is that will never happen: in the new era, the locus of control is shifting from organizations and systems to people. It is going to be more organic, more personal.

Think about what Steve Jobs and his team did at Apple. They created personalization in a whole new realm. The iPhone is not about sexy design; it is about its organic nature. Anyone who has one is in complete control of their own device. No one's device will be the same as anybody else's.

Change

The development of the App Store in particular stands out as a prime example of the temporary nature of systems, needs and life in this era. We populate our devices with applications we need right now, but it is a revolving door. Some we keep as constants – the phone element, the camera, the contacts list – but others are downloaded, used and discarded as required. When recently I flew to Australia on Emirates, I downloaded the Emirates app with its flight information, airport maps and the ability to use my phone as a boarding pass. Two weeks later I deleted it and downloaded the American Airlines equivalent for my next trip.

What we have to do is super-project that kind of philosophy into the way we live our lives, and see that we are the equivalent of living, breathing iPhones and the world is full of apps. We need to view ourselves more like a smartphone, to ground ourselves with some key skills – being literate and numerate, for example – but to anticipate and think through new situations, and to be prepared to adapt more readily than making circumstances

Refresh

fit our limitations. We must work harder to ensure we are flexible, constantly learning new skills, furnishing ourselves with new apps to remain relevant and able to respond to the needs of the world around us.

*The world is 2.0 and we are still 1.0. We need a complete reboot.*

The world is 2.0 and we are still 1.0. We need a complete reboot. We need a different kind of central processor. There are new fundamental truths which will dominate our futures, truths that require us to exist with new economic, ecological and social models, which mean that, sadly, hunkering down, putting on an Ol' Blue Eyes CD and waiting for the storm to pass is simply no longer an option.

The ability to change, on all levels, is now as fundamental to our ability to survive and thrive as is our ability to breathe.

Change

┌─────────────────────────────┐
│      Your Change App        │
├─────────────────────────────┤
│         **Refresh**         │
└─────────────────────────────┘

- The next time you hear about an advance, no matter how obscure the field, be selfish and think about its potential in your own sector of activity, your own sphere of influence.

- Follow the example of Sir Alex Ferguson: play out scenarios in your head and within the context of your life and career. What can you change to challenge yourself and those around you, to keep fresh and on your toes?

- The minute you feel comfortable, do something about it. Find a harder cushion ... It may come to nothing but the more you keep shifting outside your comfort zone, the more chance you give yourself to develop new thinking, ideas and methodologies.

- Create a bank of 'snapshot' moments that can be used to frame new nostalgia. Snapshot moments

Refresh

happen when you take a mental photograph, a way of recognizing the here and now. We do not spend enough time celebrating the moments we are in, and too often only value them much later.

● Aim to become your own internal action researcher, deconstructing and exploring what may appear to be abstracts. For example, I recently asked a cosmetics company to describe what a virtual perfume would smell like...

● Think of yourself as a human smartphone – which stale applications should you be deleting from your personal mindset and which new attitudes, systems and skills is it time to download?

Change

# BELIEVE

---

'When you create change, you can be wrong, but always believe that you are doing it for the right reasons.'

# Change

I left school hating education, resenting everything, never wanting to go back. I was angry and I was lonely. At eighteen I was thrown outside the bubble of education into a very real, confusing world for which I was even less prepared. When I finally decided to go back to college, I suddenly felt for the first time in all of my remembered life that I actually belonged somewhere.

Within that first week of starting college I appreciated the surroundings. I had made the right choice for me. I had made that choice. I was in control. I was more mature, and I found myself in an environment with people who were just like me. I remember lying on my bed in that first week, looking at the poster of Bob Marley – we all had to have Bob Marley on our walls – lying in this tiny cupboard of a room in Derby, and feeling happier than I could ever remember.

Only then did I start to realize who I was, what my passions were, what my interests were, what my strengths and weaknesses really were.

Later, as I moved into teaching as a career, I became aware how dangerous education can be in terms of limiting people's horizons and artificially boosting self-esteem to an unwarranted level.

If everything is too precise and too specific, there is little opportunity for people to work above or outside their remit; to question, challenge or investigate; to use their powers of curiosity and creativity. We all have a maverick side and sometimes we must develop strategies that work against conformity to positively encourage a little rebellion.

In his novel *The Shack*, William P. Young has

Believe

*We all have a maverick side and sometimes we must positively encourage a little rebellion.*

a lawyer remark that trying to keep the law 'grants you the power to judge others and feel superior to them. You believe you are living to a higher standard than those you judge. Enforcing rules, especially in its more subtle expressions like responsibility and expectation, is a vain attempt to create certainty out of uncertainty. And contrary to what you might think, I have a great fondness for uncertainty. Rules cannot bring freedom; they only have the power to accuse.'

Too often targets are set as a measure of expected performance, not as a tool to encourage extraordinary development.

To break this pattern, it is vital to throw in abstract questions to generate debate and discussion that is divorced from specific outcomes.

# Change

Too many meetings begin with data-driven problems: 'We have to cut costs' or 'We must increase our projected sales figures'. This is always going to result in SMART-focused discussions, which is perfectly valid if the aim is to focus on existing systems of productivity but not if the aim is to develop cultures of change and innovation. Sometimes it is important to work against perceived wisdom or the safe option.

Too many people confuse 'vision' with 'strategy', and as a result we end up with initiative overload. Too much of what we do and endeavour to implement ends up being layered on top of existing systems which leads to workforces feeling under increasing pressure, time-poor and often highly cynical.

To break that pattern requires a new mindset, a new way of thinking. Sybervision, a learning technology company, has listed what they believe are the ten common traits of truly great people:

Believe

FOCUS

PREPAREDNESS

CONVICTION

PERSEVERANCE

CREATIVITY

CURIOSITY

RESILIENCE

RISK-TAKING

INDEPENDENCE

A SENSE OF HIGHER PURPOSE

Many of the high achievers they looked at described their lives in terms of adventures, as explorations and as challenges. All of them – world-changers including Socrates, Marco Polo, Henry Ford, Copernicus, Dickens, Mozart, Monet and Gandhi – questioned convention and introduced us all to new ways of viewing the world.

Change

# Challenge for Change #3

We should be looking to develop the traits of greatness within ourselves, our people and our organizations. We must also commit to do the same for our children and young people. Wouldn't it be an entirely different type of performance management meeting if each member of your team needed to show, through specific examples, when they had demonstrated each of the traits above? Wouldn't it lead to a new direction if professional development programmes were not just about training staff to be more efficient or skilled at what they do but also to ensure that they were required to hone the traits of great people?

Believe

In my first teaching job I was able to observe what happens when people are locked into a predictable pattern of thinking. After my degree I achieved my teaching qualification and got a job in a school in inner-city Derby. This was at an interesting time in the education structure in the UK, just as the country was being given its first-ever National Curriculum during the late 1980s and early 1990s. I went into a school that was a very traditional, typical primary school, populated with teachers who had been doing the job in the same school most of their working lives, teaching the things they loved teaching, but not necessarily with any great rhyme or reason or rhythm.

So as I started my teaching career, all of a sudden a whole generation of teachers who had been more or less left to their own devices were forced to follow the very prescriptive National Curriculum imposed on schools by the government, at the same time as a new inspectorate was being formed to check on how well they were following the new order.

Change

As a young teacher I was lucky; I had been trained in the new curriculum. I walked into this school to observe a group of people who were truly lovely, who had dedicated all their lives to teaching kids, having to deal with something that was alien to them, but about which they had no choice.

I saw at first hand very early on in my working life the impact that the imposition of a will or a system had on a group of people who were not yet ready to enact it. A lot of those people became very angry and sceptical. They didn't have the energy, they didn't understand. It was not a system they were comfortable with. It wasn't the job they had loved doing for all of their lives. It wasn't what they had signed up for. Many chose to retire, and an entire generation of teachers was wiped out before their time.

If I am honest, as a newly qualified teacher I probably thought, *You crusty old codgers, for goodness' sake, get a life. Get out, let us young people have the floor.* In hindsight I realize just how frightful that must have been for them. They simply could not cope

Believe

with such an accelerated shift in control, power, system and expectation.

At the same time I found myself working alongside a member of the school's senior staff, someone who held sway at the highest level. She and I would row a great deal, especially during staff meetings. The head would allow this, but managed our conflicts carefully. Our disagreements were never personal and were always about how we could improve what we were doing; they sometimes became heated but that was because we were both passionate about the school and the children we taught. Those arguments drove the school forward because they led to fantastic ideas and processes which even now, twenty years later, would be considered innovative.

That other teacher, who went on to become an extraordinary head teacher, is now my daughter's godmother. We look back on that time and realize and appreciate the skill of the boss who framed our conflicts. We are both aware that they were some of the most exciting days of our professional lives.

# Change

On a personal level, I have much to thank her and the head teacher for, because those early experiences taught me the power of constructive conflict and encouraged me to spend my career always asking both 'What if?' *and* 'Why not?'

Maybe as a result, although I had been trained to operate within the National Curriculum, there was an instinct within me that said, 'I have got to break the rules. This is too regimented. The kids won't get this. It won't excite them.' In those early days of the National Curriculum it was easier because the inspectorial system was not yet punitive.

I had an unusual level of freedom to manipulate the system in the first few years of my teaching career; I have always been a manipulator of systems. I looked at the children I was teaching and looked at the system and thought, *I don't like this. It wouldn't work for me if I was ten, so let's play around with it.* I was allowed to be very creative even within the system.

Inside the school the perceived wisdom was

Believe

that what I was doing as a teacher was going to get me crucified at inspection time. The inspectorate came in and loved everything I was doing because they could see the basics were there but what I had done was translate the curriculum and transfer the power to the children and myself. We had a highly creative classroom environment. In my first OFSTED inspection as a teacher, in 1995, I was classified with what remains one of the highest scores of any teacher inspected in Britain under the system.

I had looked at the system and asked myself what the essentials were and how I could manipulate them for the real audience – my students. After the OFSTED inspection I grew in confidence. I was identified by both the school and the local education authority as a future star and so had opportunities given to me that most young teachers do not have. After four years, as senior teacher I had become part of the school's management team.

Partly because of the way my own thinking had

Change

evolved, and also because of those opportunities, I was able to develop and grow.

I think back to those older teachers who, confronted with the threat of the National Curriculum, had simply cut and run. Change will never happen if you are not prepared to alter your thinking. And to do that you need to create space. Change does not have to, and perhaps cannot, happen in a mad panic. The greatest change takes time. It is organic, grows, evolves. It should be never-ending.

*Change does not have to, and perhaps cannot, happen in a mad panic. The greatest change takes time.*

Outside my working life I do a lot of sitting, listening to music, staring out of the window. A couple of years ago I ran the London marathon for a charity. I was having to train by running thirty to forty miles a week and that was some of the most valuable thinking time I have ever had. It almost becomes meditative after the first couple of miles; you tune out and go to a different place.

Believe

I came up with more ideas and fresh thinking by keeping my mind off the physical pain. I also love taking the train. People say, 'You must be able to got lots of work done on the train'. The truth is I don't. I often just sit and drift.

## SPACE INVADERS

Creating that space is something companies can actively encourage. In the UK offices of both Microsoft and Google the overriding sense is of that Californian, open-office mentality, but even so they have had to create sanctuaries. So Microsoft has created pods within the wide-open spaces. If you have just arrived on a flight from the West Coast there is a space you can relax and recover in, or during the working day you can take time out and use a pod for personal reflection.

In the corporate environment most offices are still very mechanistic, the typing pool situation, where you can talk to each other and see what your colleagues are doing all the time. But you have

Change

*You have your most creative moments when you are up a mountain, on a bicycle, running, by a beach, when your brain is zoned out, as far away from work as you can ever be.*

your most creative moments when you are up a mountain, on a bicycle, running, by a beach, when your brain is zoned out, as far away from work as you can ever be. It is at precisely that moment you always have the most stunning idea.

Pixar, the legendary animated film producer, have set up a university within the company so staff can go off and explore areas of personal interest that have nothing to do with their working lives. At the Microsoft offices in Reading there is a boating lake in the middle of the campus. What they say to their people is, 'If you're stuck on something, grab one of the rowboats and go sit in the middle of the lake and look at the sky.' Because Microsoft know that is most likely to be how and when they will solve the problem. If it is

Believe

all about time and motion, about efficiency, where is the time and space to allow people to have those moments in which the nugget will emerge?

All through the twentieth century we were driven into believing that if somebody is daydreaming they are doing so at the expense of productivity, when actually what companies like Google and Facebook and Microsoft and Pixar know is that it is those moments which increase productivity, as long as they are constructed in the right way and then managed correctly.

In the same manner we have developed a cultural belief around our constant desire to find the silver bullet. Everyone assumes that in this short-term, quick-fix environment we will find the bullet and buy it in.

We have got to stop looking for the silver bullets, because they just get in the way. They create scepticism, resentment, anger. They disenfranchise people because they assume the boss is going to come in with the silver bullet anyway, so there is no point in having any original thought.

# Change

## GOING ASTRAY

When I first became head of Grange School near
Derby, I found that the staff and pupils there had
become used to a succession of people entering the
front doors ready to tell them what to do, to deliver
a new system or strategy for them to implement.
The cupboards were full of old strategy documents,
silver bullets that had missed the target. There was
no passion, no vision, no hope.

The school had become scared of doing the
wrong thing in the wrong way. The strategy needed
to be stripped back, redefined and focused to create
a sense of higher purpose, something that people
could sign up to, take control of and feel passionate
about.

The inventor and creative theorist Roger von
Oech says that it is 'important for the explorer to
be willing to be led astray'. We need to be prepared
to be led to unknown places, to appear to break the
rules, conventions and expectations. In my work
as a head teacher that idea became irresistible.

Believe

Not going beyond the garden gate was not an option. My staff may often have wondered if I was leading them astray, but they were confident enough to know that the person doing the leading believed that there was something special at the end of the pathway, something he was prepared to stake his reputation and career on.

Step one was to find a moral purpose that could act as a vision, a call to arms and a yardstick by which we could measure and audit what we were achieving. The answer was elegant and simple, a question: 'But is it right for our kids?' It was a question we could use to interrogate anyone who wanted to criticize or control. We would challenge our own ideas. We had to prove that any idea would make life better for the kids. If not, it was not going to happen. That provided the way forward, and gave us a sense of higher purpose when we were questioned by sceptics, researchers, educational experts or inspection teams.

As a public speaker, I try to stick to the same principles. It can be scary standing up there on a

Change

stage, under lights, under scrutiny, particularly when I am talking about sensitive and challenging concepts such as education and politics. I am putting my head high up over the parapet, an easy target for anyone who would like to take a pot shot. I will never be able to please everybody in an audience. There will always be someone who disagrees, who is offended by my stance or who does not want to hear what I have to say. I will speak only if I can talk about the topic from my heart, with belief and conviction.

I never claim to possess all the answers – I am honest about that – but I plan to provoke thinking and am clear that my thoughts are my beliefs. In that way I hope that people will respect my integrity, even if they don't agree with me.

I had a special relationship with my maternal grandfather. When he died I was deeply affected, but an event at his funeral proved to be an epiphany for me. After he had been laid to rest, I was standing by the graveside lost in my own thoughts. One of my grandfather's closest friends

Believe

and oldest business associates came up to me, put his hand on my shoulder and said, 'He was a special man, a man of real integrity.' I thought how great a legacy that was, to live your life with your integrity intact. That is my thinking precisely.

Change

# Believe

• Take time to think of yourself as a brand. If you were a brand what would you be and what would you want to be? This may vary in different contexts: work, home, leisure. Use the classic branding lens to monitor your outward image – what do I want to stand for in the eyes of others, and how does my behaviour reflect that?

• Always challenge your own actions and thinking – ask yourself, 'Am I doing what I am doing because it has integrity? Have I really explored the possibilities of what I believe in or am I accepting an easier option?' Don't sell yourself short, but only take a punt when it really matters to you.

Believe

● If you are leading others, that is your challenge: you must create the route that connects and matters to all of them.

● If you are being led, challenge your leaders to make their thinking compulsive. Force them to communicate and sell it to you.

Change

# QUESTION

---

'I live in a world of personal action research: have an idea, work it through until it feels right, and give it a go. Then analyse the results.'

# Change

The first genuine opportunity I had to put into practice the ideas that were starting to brew inside my head as a young teacher was when I was appointed head teacher of Grange School.

After five years as a teacher, and having received such a strong recommendation from the OFSTED inspectors, I had been made deputy head of a large primary school in Derbyshire, from where I was poached three and a half years later by the local authority because they wanted me to run a project with disaffected children.

They asked me to work with kids, boys in

particular, who came from complex and difficult situations and who were seriously demotivated, particularly when it came to producing written work. For me that was all about transferring power to the children: how do you get the kids to *choose* to want to write, how do you stimulate that choice? It was invaluable experience in understanding how to encourage them away from believing they had to sit with their heads down and do what they were told and instead construct a powerful and creative environment: exactly the same attitude I now try and stimulate among people at work.

I left there in 2001 to become head of Grange School at Long Eaton, between Nottingham and Derby. I remember being briefed about the school by the local government department: I was told that Grange had 'seen much better days', that it had been in decline for some time and that the staff, pupils and buildings were tired. Fired up by this enthusiastic and highly motivational analysis, I headed off looking for a building with a permanent cloud hanging over its leaking roof.

Question

As I walked through the gates of the school and down a long path towards the main building, it felt as if I was walking home. You know that sense you get when you are in the market for a new house; you trawl through the estate agents' details, you visit a few which feel soulless until finally you strike gold.

You view a property, much the same as all the others you've viewed, in the same area and with all the same proportions, but for some reason, for some ethereal reason, you know you belong there. Suddenly you can see the Christmas tree in the living room, imagine the children charging down the stairs and into the kitchen in search of food.

That is exactly how I felt as I entered Grange School's main building through its vast wooden doors. I didn't see the 'difficult' staff or the 'unteachable' children. I just knew that this was a place where I could belong. I spent a good hour talking to the acting head (the real one had been off sick for some time) and by the time she showed

Change

me back to the gates, I was determined to apply for the job that she clearly didn't want.

My determination was fired because I could feel the potential in the place: in her, in the staff and, most importantly, in the children. By the time I had returned to my office, I had already made up my mind to tell my boss and to put in a formal application. I was shortlisted for interview – no great achievement, as there were only three applicants – but when I arrived, ready to be put through the selection meetings, I realized that I was by far the least experienced of the candidates. In hindsight, I think that that helped. I got the job.

I learned later that the appointment board had been desperate to appoint someone with vision. They were looking for a candidate who could offer inspiration to the school; through the couple of days of the interview and assessment process I had been able to project that quite strongly. They told me that I lacked some experience and some of the requisite technical know-how, but I would have an

Question

*The chair of the board of governors asked me what I imagined the school would be like and I said, 'Like a Disneyland of learning.'*

experienced deputy in place who would help me to plug that gap.

The clincher, as it turned out, was when the chair of the board of governors asked me what I imagined the school would be like if I were running it and I said, 'Like a Disneyland of learning.' I meant it, too. I had just come back from a trip there with my own children and I had seen the awe and wonder it generated, the fact that fidgety young children were prepared to queue for hours, for maybe two or three minutes of magic. My answer was not a systemic response, based on policies and implementation, it was a picture, something emotive and tangible and what that school community needed at that particular moment in time ... Thank you, Walt.

## Change

By the time I took on the job I had acquired –
thanks to my teaching experience and my time
working for the local authority – everything
I needed to know about giving people the power
to change things for themselves and what that can
lead to in terms of outcome and success. When
I became a head I was able to apply throughout
the school, to staff and pupils alike, all the lessons
I had learned from being a teacher in a classroom
with tough children.

Some of the most frustrating and stifling
conflicts in organizations occur when the declared
ethos is one of innovation and change but the
systems of accountability are fixed points of
measurable performance. At Grange School, it was
very hard to sell a vision for the future that was
all about the development of organic and creative
cultures when the school was being held to account
in such narrow ways. The scales of risk were
always going to be tipped in favour of the option
that represented certainty and self-preservation,
amplified, of course, by the fact that it was a 'failing

Question

school' that could relieve the pressure building on it only by demonstrating a rapid rise in short-term measurable outcomes.

## OBSTACLE COURSE

The first task I faced was not just to communicate a vision for the future but to remove the obstacles that stood in the way of developing it. That meant finding new forms of accountability that kept the staff feeling secure but did not limit their potential or allow them to reside in the protection of a 'just enough' culture. One of the first things I did was to change the performance management and professional development strategies.

In terms of managing performance, we were required by law to set three targets, one of which we applied the SMART target approach to. That, the 'professional' target, was based on the measurable outcomes of the students in one particular area, identified within a cohort, for example mathematical equations.

Change

The second target, the 'personal' target, was defined by each member of staff based on the list of traits of successful people. They defined the actions they would take to evolve those traits, which did not necessarily need to take place during the working week but could be supported by any part of their lives.

And the third, the 'growth' target, was a requirement for each member of staff to develop a new skill or to live through a new experience, which need not have any direct relation to the job they did. This third target was vital in developing in the staff a sense of a world beyond the job that they did, since it stimulated their own curiosity and creative process.

I needed to put all that in place because the level of change I had in mind for the school was radical in terms of convention and expectation. We destroyed the National Curriculum, and people on the outside looked at us and said it would never work. But it did. We had two OFSTED inspections under that system and the inspectorate loved it.

Question

In constructing a way of operating I had not broken a single element of curricular legislation.

We got rid of traditional subject teaching: instead of delivering bog-standard lessons in history, geography, music, art, English, maths and science, we created a four-stranded curriculum. My idea was that there should be no such thing as stand-alone disciplines, that disciplines are cross-connected. So I asked the question, 'How do you link content with disciplines in a world that is contextual for kids?'

In response I came up with four concepts – communication, enterprise, culture and well-being – as the four cornerstones of twenty-first-century society. I still don't know where that idea came from: it was probably an instinctive reaction to how I lived my life, which was based around being a capable communicator, having a spirit of entrepreneurship and enterprise, possessing a real interest in culture – not just the arts but all forms of culture – and also knowing that all of that can only be possible if you truly understand what well-being means to you and you endeavour to create the conditions for well-being.

This was not a ready-made theory plucked out of an academic thesis or a how-to book. I trusted my instincts. I often describe myself as instinctive. When people ask me questions about professional and personal decision-making, I tell them that they will 'feel' when they are on the right path. Sometimes, in my more altruistic moments, I tell people that I have been lucky in my life, that the successes I've had have resulted from being in the right place at the right time, but, between you and me, I am not sure that is entirely true. I often wonder whether we all have luck; it is just a question of being able to recognize the moment and then having the courage or vision to seize it.

*It is just a question of being able to recognize the moment and then having the courage or vision to seize it.*

Question

My challenge at Grange was twofold. If I was going to create a new curriculum for the children, how could I articulate to other people something that I had evolved internally? Previously I had been toiling away happily in my own little bubble. A class teacher works in a precisely defined environment: the classroom. Translating that to a group of different people in different contexts and then trying to get them to implement the change, *there* was the challenge.

## LIVING, LEARNING, LAUGHING

I had to define what I stood for as a teacher in as straightforward and direct language as I could. I refined and refined the central message until I came down to three core words: living, learning and laughing.

My message to the staff at Grange School was, 'I don't care how you do it, but when I walk around this school as its head, I want to feel that the children have a sense they are living their lives, and that by engaging in school they are going to learn to live it better. That it is all about learning, but not just learning to fulfil some abstract future goal, but actually learning things that have a resonance and a magic for the moment. And in doing that, the school should be filled with the right kind of laughter.' What I meant by that was everyone should be relaxed enough to be themselves.

As the head of Grange, my aim was not to impose a course the school must follow but to create the conditions for people to have their *own* visualizations, to have their own thinking, to know that there was an agreed core purpose. My role was also to remind everybody about what we were there for, what our values were, what made our hearts beat faster.

At the school the main driving force for us was  the children: they were at the heart of everything. I wanted the teaching staff to have the confidence to play with ideas and then tell me what they were thinking. I promised them that if

Question

we could find some communality we would work it up and try it out.

This is the essence of everything I have carried into the role of leadership. Professor Bernard Bass of the University of New York has identified and described two kinds of leader, his definitions of which are useful touchstones. A **transactional leader**, he says, is someone who:

- contracts exchange of rewards for effort, promises rewards for good performance, recognizes accomplishments;

- watches and searches for deviations from rules and standards, takes corrective action;

- intervenes only if standards are not met;

- abdicates responsibilities, avoids making decisions.

In contrast there is what Professor Bass calls a **transformational leader**, someone who:

- provides vision and a sense of mission, instils pride, gains respect and trust;

Change

- communicates high expectations, uses symbols to focus efforts and expresses important purposes in simple ways;

- promotes intelligence, rationality and careful problem solving; gives personal attention, treats each employee individually, coaches, advises.

The chef Ferran Adrià represents a great example of a transformational leader. He was founder and head chef of El Bulli, the restaurant on the Costa Brava widely lauded as the world's finest, famed for its groundbreaking, innovative approach to cooking. In February 2012, after building the business from scratch and turning it into the most successful and celebrated operation in its field, Ferran Adrià shut El Bulli down, at the height of its success.

Adrià had always challenged convention and was one of the first chefs to explore the application of advanced science, through the use of chemistry and psychology, to his cooking (inspiring, among others, the extraordinary Heston Blumenthal). The

Question

decision to close El Bulli was the result of Adrià's desire to move beyond the pressures of running a restaurant to explore his culinary art and expand the food laboratory he had always run alongside the restaurant. Aficionados were shocked by his decision, but in truth it was not surprising, given his iconoclastic character.

His new centre, El Taller, is a fluid facility that promotes collaboration, bringing together chefs, scientists and experts from seemingly disconnected backgrounds to continue his deconstruction of convention. He will ask these newly formed teams an open-ended philosophical question: perhaps 'What is soup?' or 'Is flavour just about taste?' and see what happens. But Ferran Adrià is no middle-aged hippy. He is demanding and challenging, a perfectionist who works with the precision and detail of a research scientist, analysing, question-ing, processing and recording his work.

As a transformational leader, he heads a team in one of the most competitive, high-pressure markets, and in the process has built a

Change

multinational multimillion-euro business. His vision is core to his success, his uncompromising values an inspiration to all who work with him or have been influenced by him. His inner instinct has been to empower others to help him achieve his vision through their own unique skills and talents. If he had been a transactional rather than transformational leader he would probably have ended up running McDonald's, where consistency of the product is central to the business's success, the same taste day in day out, from LA to London or Ljubljana.

Question

# Challenge for Change #4

Can we find those same open-ended questions in our own business, our own sector, our own area of activity? They are powerful tools for transformation, encouraging discussion and debate, stimulating curiosity and exploration.

I saw the results of the transformational approach in a direct way very shortly after I started working at Grange School. I was in the first week of my time there, doing what everyone does when they start a leadership role in a new company: interviewing the entire staff. The lovely thing about being a new leader is that when you ask, 'What do you think of the place?' it is the only time the staff will ever be honest with you. They can be brutally truthful because they know that as a new leader you don't own the previous situation and will not mind what they say.

Change

I went through all the staff and met this one guy, George. He had been teaching in the school more or less all his professional life, and lived in the community. He came into my office, said, 'Richard, I know you are the new head. I appreciate you want to do really good things for this school, so I want to let you know I will do what you ask me to do but I won't do any more than that because I've done my time, I've done my share of out-of-hours and extra-curricular work. I am just working towards my retirement.' I asked him, 'If you don't mind me asking, how old are you?' 'I'm forty-eight,' he said. Well, that was a problem, because as a teacher you didn't retire until sixty-five minimum. With seventeen more years to go he had decided he was not going to do more than toe the line.

Later that week, I happened to be in the staffroom and overheard George holding court in a Victor Meldrew moment. He was having a bit of a moan to some of his colleagues: 'If my father hadn't been so lousy with money I wouldn't be here now, I'd be running the shop. All I wanted to

Question

do is run the family business . . .' And that was when the thought struck me, *Oh my God, that is what makes him tick.*

I left the thought to one side for a couple of days, because it would have been too obvious if I had immediately said, 'George, could I have a word now?' When I asked him to come and see me, of course the first thing he said was, 'What have I done wrong?' I said, 'I hope you don't mind, but I overheard a conversation you were having about a shop . . .' And with that prompt he poured everything out about what he had wanted to do with the family store.

At the time I was evolving the idea of the school containing its own 'town' run by the pupils, with a council and mayor, and including a restaurant, TV and radio stations and a museum. I asked George how he would feel about setting up a shop as part of the town, and then training the kids to run it. I said I would be happy to send him on some professional retail training courses.

And his eyes lit up. 'What, really?' 'Yes.' 'Would

Change

I have complete control?' 'Absolutely. You tell me what you need and want and it's yours.' That one conversation completely transformed who George was and how he behaved. He took control of the project, he took ownership of it, and within a couple of years we had promoted him to a position as part of the senior management team, and he became incredibly supportive of everything we were trying to do. That was transformation in action in the most uplifting and visible way.

Question

> ### Your Change App
> # Question

- Even if you are on your own, ask yourself the questions a child might ask: 'Why is the sky blue?' 'What would happen if...?'

- Question yourself regularly, the more abstract the better. Nurture and develop curiosity in yourself, and others, to ensure a transformational mindset.

- Transform your daily activity. Dreaming about change is fine, but putting it into practice is the only way to make it happen.

- Make a list of your interests, your passions, the things you enjoy. Look at how you can deploy those attributes in other areas of your life.

# VISUALIZE

---

'Vision is vitally important individually
and professionally for all of us, not just
those who are paid to lead.'

# Change

When I was a teenager I had the opportunity to meet a true visionary. When David Hockney first moved to London, he rented a flat from my grandfather, who owned a few properties in London. At the time Hockney was an art student; nobody really knew about him yet and often he had no money to pay the rent – instead he paid in sketches and paintings. My grandfather loved the arts, although he was never able to understand Hockney's work and never thought he would be a success (and sadly didn't keep the sketches or paintings he was given). However he respected him as an artist and thought he was a nice kid.

Hockney eventually left the flat but he and my grandfather always stayed in touch because Hockney recognized that my grandfather had been deeply generous, and he never forgot that. While my grandfather was alive, whenever Hockney came back from LA, he would always invite him to his studios just off Portobello Road, where he used to come for six weeks every summer. One year, when I was quite young, maybe twelve or thirteen, and I was very involved in art and painting, my grandfather asked, 'Can I bring my grandson along to meet you? I know he would love it.' Hockney said, 'Yes, why don't you ask him to bring his portfolio with him?'

So I did. I took along my portfolio of art – which was competent, but no more than that – and David Hockney spent two and a half hours with me going through my paintings. As a child of twelve or thirteen, I knew he was a famous artist but not much more. And he was positive, constructive and

Visualize

creative. 'You want to be an artist, Richard, go for it, make it happen and in another few years come back and show me what you have done.' His enthusiasm, his example, his encouragement to act, the sharing of his vision has stayed with me to this day.

So much of what we do or don't achieve is because of a lack of vision or the inability to believe in it or act upon it. How many people have had an inspirational moment in the shower that gets washed away with the soap and water? A dream that fades in the sunlight?

A vision is not a neat and tidy animal; it cannot be designed on a boardroom table or found in a self-help manual. To be authentic it must come from a belief, a sense, an idea. It is often something that nags inside you and becomes so insistent that you must act upon it.

*A vision is often something that nags inside you and becomes so insistent that you must act upon it.*

As a leader within an organization, particularly when times are tough, when change and uncertainty reign, it is so important to recognize the responsibility of service that you carry. One of the great arts of leadership is to serve the people who work for and with you. That is a lesson I learned as a teacher, because the greatest teachers serve the needs of their children – and sometimes that means pointing to the stars rather than looking at your feet. It requires you to value and nurture your vision, your passion.

Charles Handy, the organizational guru, says that those companies which survive for longest are 'the ones that work out what they uniquely can give to the world – not just growth or money but their excellence, their respect for others, or their ability to make people happy. Some call those things a soul.' His choice of the word 'soul' interests me most because it says something about humanity: a personal insight, an honesty, qualities that I think define the power of a vision. It is an essential part of what Bernard Bass defined as 'transformational' (rather than 'transactional') leadership.

In many ways, transactional leadership is a product of the past, harking back to Taylorism.

Visualize

It creates a sense of efficiency and productivity that is particularly appealing in times of crisis because the perception at these times is that there is no space for thinking forward or for innovation, that survival depends on cutting costs and breaking even. Of course the time for inspirational leadership is *exactly* at that point, because it is then that the feeling of powerlessness, of victim culture, starts to creep into the psyche.

Too often individuals and organizations only seriously consider change when they are going through hard times. Most people are happy doing what they have always done; transactional thinking is familiar and the safest way to go. It is transformative thinkers, though, who change the world.

It was Robert F. Kennedy who, in his plea to humanity, said, 'Many of the world's great movements, of thought and action, have flowed from the work of a single man. A young monk began the Protestant reformation, a young general extended an empire from Macedonia to the borders of the earth, and a young woman reclaimed the

# Change

territory of France. It was a young Italian explorer who discovered the New World, and thirty-two-year-old Thomas Jefferson who proclaimed that all men are created equal. "Give me a place to stand," said Archimedes, "and I will move the world." These men moved the world, and so can we all.'

On 20 January 2009 I was watching the television with a lump in my throat and the feeling you get when you know you are observing history in the making. I insisted that my daughter, then aged twelve, came and sat next to me in our living room. Together we watched as Barack Obama was inaugurated as the 44th President of the United States of America.

I have always been drawn to communicators, possibly because, as a child, I envied their use of language, their ability to persuade, inspire and demand attention. I was captivated by the oratory of Martin Luther King Jr, and for obvious reasons his words came right back to me in the moment I watched a black American accept the presidency, the fruition of Martin Luther King's dream.

Visualize

Great orators are so skilled at presenting a vision that is tangible because of its clarity and connection to people, their thoughts carefully moulded to create a call to action in those who hear it. The listeners respond because they are ready to follow. There is no implied threat or insistence on a fait accompli. The speech has found a resonance with their personal contexts, which results in the need to act.

*Vision cannot break through when you are busy doing what you have always done.*

One thing is more than clear: the greatest people, the greatest organizations, are always looking to the future, they are always analysing their position and where they can go next.

One of the most important factors in the ability to develop a vision is to be able to raise your head above the parapet, to push yourself constantly, to explore new things, to encounter new experiences and stimulate new thinking. Vision cannot break through when you are busy doing what you have always done.

## Change

# Challenge for Change #5

Once you have developed a vision, taken it from that instinctive nagging stab to something that you can feel and get excited about, how can you sell that vision to others?

Visualize

A couple of years ago I came across the German word *Rückwärtslaufen*. Some call it 'Retro locomotion'. It's basically running backwards. Apparently, this is kinder on your joints than conventional running but brings with it dangers all of its own, especially, one would imagine, bumping into things.

I have to confess that when I first heard about this technique I tried it but it felt so alien and unfamiliar that I soon turned to face forward. I didn't like not being able to see what was coming. I reverted to type and have since stuck to what I know, good old running forward. I have worked on my efficiency, bought better trainers, added knee supports and found a new stride pattern but I am still doing what I have always done.

However, if I had found an expert, someone who was passionate about *Rückwärtslaufen*, who could have coached me, reassured me and above all sold me the vision as well as giving me the skills and direction to develop my confidence, I might well have stuck at it.

# Change

Selling your vision is much like building a brand. The American Branding Association defines a brand as 'the personality that identifies a product, service or company and how it relates to key constituencies: customers, staff, partners, investors etc. Some people distinguish the psychological aspect, brand associations like thoughts, feelings, perceptions, images, experiences, beliefs, attitudes and so on, that become linked to the brand, of a brand from the experiential aspect.'

As thinking about brand development has evolved over the last few decades, brand marketeers have moved towards a more emotive and experiential language. Brands are now all about lifestyle, and it strikes me that the same principles need to be applied in communicating a vision. It is a skilled and developmental process, not something you can 'present' at a convened meeting on a Monday morning around the boardroom table with coffee, Krispy Kremes, a bowl of fruit for show and some PowerPoint slides lovingly crafted to cross-fade and dissolve.

Visualize

## NURTURE, PROVOKE

One of the greatest frustrations I detect from many of the leaders I meet is the number of times they communicate a vision, only to see it reside in the cupboard full of new initiatives and ideas that is the graveyard of hope.

A vision must be nurtured. This can take time, which is counter-intuitive when the vision is so clear in your own head. We are motivated to move forward because we can see the challenge, the problem and the ambition as our responsibility. The frustration comes when you expect others to chant, 'But of course, we must start right away!' The reality is sometimes consensus, and sometimes confusion, but very rarely momentum.

In order to disseminate the value of your vision, you must work hard to provoke people's thinking. Communicating a vision must not start with your response but the catalyst that led you to go on the journey – you need to provoke emotive responses in others.

Change

While presenting a vision to a group can be a start, the real impact can only happen through one-to-one conversations, personal contact and the individual nurturing of each person's situation. Perception of your vision by others is often

*Tapping into that emotional drive is what will propel other people to change.*

hampered by the perception of the motivation for communicating it now. A vision cannot be reactive; it must be proactive. Because of the challenges the West has been facing economically and the radical rethinking and restructuring which that has led to, most of the current thinking on change is that change has been brought about by matters beyond our control. As a result, reactive responses to change and the defining of a new vision become rich pickings for the cynics.

That is why the investment of time and commitment into the development of an ethos is so important. It is simply not enough to ask people to come together and collaborate in tough

Visualize

times after decades of being encouraged to work competitively when the milk and honey were flowing. Developing cultures of empowerment and collaboration are vital for any group of people if there is to be a genuine transference of vision into action.

Western culture too often demands that the workplace needs to be coldly logical and not somewhere where emotion has a place. This goes against the branding philosophy of modern times: the Holy Grail for a brand strategy is to provoke feelings in people; you only have to watch an episode of *The X Factor* to know its success lies in the fact that every episode will try to make you cry, smile, laugh and rant. Brand specialists understand that the critical question is whether the right emotional responses will be evoked, because people will become hooked on the vision when they can feel it too.

Tapping into that emotional drive is what will propel other people to change. It is what happened when I offered George the chance to set up and

Change

run the shop that became a central part of the Grangeton experiment at Grange School. As part of the same project I was able to help another teacher to unleash her own vision – appropriately, because hers was for the school to have its own television studios.

One of my younger teachers, Jen, had a degree in media studies and had worked for a while at the BBC as a researcher for a hard-hitting investigative journalist. But she had also trained as a teacher, and that had drawn her back into the education system. I knew when we appointed her that she was highly talented and that life offered her many possibilities. My challenge was to allow her to find what would keep her at Grange. I needed to make sure she had something really gristy that was at the heart of her passion.

She came into my office one day and said, 'Richard, why don't we have a television studio so the kids can make television programmes?' I smiled and said, 'That's a great idea,' even though underneath I was rather taken aback at her

Visualize

effrontery. But as I was driving home in the evening I stopped feeling aggrieved and thought, *That is actually very cool.*

My journey home was a good one. I always had at least half an hour in the car driving from school to home so I would work things out en route. The television studio became an idea that stuck. Then it turned into, 'We couldn't possibly ... How would we do it, where would the money come from? And if she left in six months, it would all fall flat ...'

The really liberating thing for me as a leader was the realization that it was not my problem. The mistake that people in management-leadership positions frequently make is they think it is their job to make things happen, but I developed a very laissez-faire view. I realized that all I needed to do was go back in the next day and say, 'Look, Jen, I will help you however I can. You have given yourself a project, make it happen.' It freed me of responsibility for the idea's success or failure, and of course she delivered. She would come to me and say, 'Do you know anyone at the local TV

Change

*Freeing up people is a real leadership art: you want to free them, but at the same time ensure that there is a genuine link back to the core purpose, aim and vision.*

station who can help because we need to talk to them?' 'Leave it with me, Jen. You go back to your classroom, come and see me again at break and I promise I will have phoned them and we'll see if we can cook up a meeting.'

Freeing up people is so tricky, a real leadership art: you want to free them, but at the same time ensure that there is a genuine link back to the core purpose, aim and vision. It certainly worked for Jen. She stayed at the school for five years.

Jen's experience is valuable not just because of the way she embraced the spirit of the Grange School vision, but because it in turn allows me to convey the importance of vision through her story. The American priest and theologian Matthew Fox wrote this about storytelling and education: 'I am

Visualize

struck by how important storytelling is among tribal peoples; it forms the basis of their educational systems. The Celtic peoples, for example, insisted that only the poets could be teachers. Why? I think it is because knowledge that is not passed through the heart is dangerous: it may lack wisdom; it may be a power trip; it may squelch life out of the learners. What if our educational systems were to insist that teachers be poets and storytellers and artists? What transformations would follow?'

For most of my own life I have found that the logical arguments that are necessary to support a vision are the most difficult, as I am an instinctive person. I think from the heart but sometimes that is not enough, particularly if you are operating in a high-pressure environment where results rightly matter. A vision must lead to an outcome that can be judged and accountable, but that doesn't mean that it needs to end up on a spreadsheet.

In my work as a speaker I make sure I am not merely lecturing, but using stories as tools to build

Change

momentum in others. Stories have a powerful, emotive impact that is impossible to match.

## MEASURING UP

To measure my success in communicating my vision, or holding my leadership to account, I have always used a three-stage method. It is an easy, useful way of interrogating the impact you are having.

The successful realization of a vision depends on your ability to communicate it to others, to do it in such a way that it not only motivates but actually empowers them, provoking them to action and giving them the confidence, trust, belief and opportunities they need – and finally that you have clear outcomes that you can use to measure the impact of your leadership and your thinking.

You can work through those three stages: (1) *Have I communicated effectively?* (2) *Do others feel ready to take responsibility for the action that needs to follow?* And as a result, (3) *Am I seeing the impact in the realization of my vision?*

Visualize

At Grange School I had to convince some members of staff that we needed to make dramatic changes to the way we worked. I started one of my first meetings as head teacher by telling the team that we were failing our children: not because they were not getting the exam results they wanted, but because the children saw school as a form of purgatory rather than pleasure. I said that for kids to spend the best part of their waking lives in that kind of atmosphere was only going to develop resentment and failure.

I selected specific children and talked about how we were failing them: the child we had excused because he had recently lost a parent and as a result should be allowed to zone out in class. And the children we were condemning because of their behaviour, when I would challenge the staff to ask themselves what in their lessons was worth behaving for. I knew it was working because those same people would volunteer new ideas and, even better, invite me in to see those ideas in practice.

Change

My words certainly struck a chord and the debate that followed – both formal and outside my earshot – began to stir people. Willingly or otherwise, they were active participants in the journey to follow. They became integral to the process of transforming the school.

Visualize

> ## Your Change App
> # Visualize

- Take an issue you are passionate about, find an emotive story that best exemplifies not only the point you want to make but also how you are feeling. Use that as a foundation the next time you have to convince someone of your position, belief or direction of travel.

- Dr Alex Lickerman, a physician and practising Buddhist, has a list of reminders to himself when he is faced with trying something new:

  1. Trying something new requires courage.

  2. Trying something new opens up the possibility of enjoying something new.

  3. Trying something new keeps you from boredom.

  4. Trying something new forces you to grow.

- To ensure momentum for change both personally and professionally, work on those four levers. In the

Change

same way that regular exercise keeps us physically fit, creating regular opportunities to experience each of those attributes will strengthen your abilities (and those of the people who work with you) by keeping your vision fresh. You will be far more likely to create a dynamic, transformational and organic organization.

● Apply the three-stage process of holding your own leadership to account. Give yourself a checklist. Are you communicating your vision? Is it provoking others to action, and giving them the confidence, trust and belief they need? And have you got clear outcomes you can use to measure the impact of your leadership and thinking?

Visualize

Change

# SHARE

'People need people. That is why
change cannot be successful
if it is tackled alone.'

# Change

As a teacher I would often stand in my classroom tearing my hair out, desperate to find a way to reach a certain child or to inspire another. I would look out of the large windows at the fields and the life beyond and feel that I was isolated in my own personal challenge.

Later, as a school leader, I would do the same when confronted with budget cuts, high-pressure targets, angry parents and difficult staff. Sometimes I would stare at an aggressive letter from an anxious mother and wish I could be doing someone else's job in a less complex world.

Dynamic people are able to overcome that sense of isolation through collaborating with others, and by realizing that we all face similar problems, both personal and professional. We are only alone if we want to be; we must get out more, share more and achieve more... together.

*I make it a rule to check out every email, every initial contact, and to catch up with as many of those as possible.*

Time is as critical an element in the development of new partnerships as the ability to trust one's instinct. I go out of my way to look for the new experiences that meeting and networking can bring. I make it a rule to check out every email, every initial contact, and to catch up with as many of those as possible. I am a social animal. I love being in the company of others, of hearing others' stories, of sharing their triumphs, their failures, their dreams and their dilemmas.

I suppose that much of my reputation as an innovator and creative leader arose from my work at Grange School, but I have always told people that it

Share

was not *my* creativity that changed that place. It was the collective power of all the people involved in the school.

Of course I had a strong vision and belief. I had ideas. But you cannot thrive alone. Innovation and creativity, in order to be realized, are collaborative processes. The most important personal and professional growth cannot take place in isolation; we need to be stimulated, challenged and supported.

As the extraordinary American poet and activist Mattie Stepanek said shortly before he died, a month before his fourteenth birthday, 'Unity is strength . . . When there is teamwork and collaboration, wonderful things can be achieved.'

Much of that collaboration can be driven by simply talking to each other: the incredible power of dialogue. The important thing in terms of being able to find out who you are is to be able to talk it through with people. In my experience very few people do that.

Communication is vital. It has to be collegiate,

Change

has to be collaborative. My personal eureka moment was that cliché of sitting around with a group of people who were on my degree course. I often say that some of the best times in my life were those nights at two in the morning, post-kebab, sitting there with a candle and a joss stick and just talking. That element of higher education is valuable to everybody, those soft, unplanned, snatched moments when people work through their own thinking, about who they are and what they are in a comfort zone. We should remember that throughout our supposedly grown-up, professional lives.

When I moved into school management, I did remember that. One of the most crucial things about the development of Grange was the space and time for people to talk freely, to throw in abstract concepts, daft questions like 'Why isn't school like Disneyland?', 'How do we create a marketing campaign to sell school to children?' All those big-thinking questions.

Ironically, it often appears that when we need

Share

people the most – in times of trouble and uncertainty – we tend to retreat inside ourselves, like a snail into its shell. I have heard many stories of leaders and managers who take problems upon themselves, who assume personal responsibility for finding solutions and then as the situations deteriorate, become increasingly isolated and stressed. At a point when clarity and perspective become vital, their heads are fogged with stress and pressure, making finding solutions almost impossible and the chances of creative problem-solving minimal. I have worked for people like this, good people, skilled, intelligent, moral leaders, who have sunk under the weight of their own isolation.

*Too much stress on an individual results in a lack of motivation and creativity.*

Too much stress on an individual results in a lack of motivation and creativity. That is why the building and nurturing of relationships is so important and worth fighting for, even when people feel at their most exposed or vulnerable. It is also

Change

true to say that we must commit to exploring new collaborations, partnerships and friendships and, in doing so, remember that some of the most innovative ideas come from conflict.

During my teacher training, I came across a quote by Robert Fulghum, which I still love to pass on: 'We could learn a lot from crayons: some are sharp, some are pretty, some are dull, while others are bright, some have weird names, but we have to learn to live in the same box.' Our instinct is to group ourselves with people we perceive as having similar interests, statuses, beliefs and attitudes. How often at work do you pull away from the awkward voice, the dissenter, when they could be the very person with whom collaboration could be the most exciting?

'There is nothing better for self-growth than somebody challenging your own viewpoint.'

Share

When I am talking to large corporates, my message is: 'One of your biggest problems is that when you are filling a vacancy in a department, you are looking for somebody who will fit in and be just like everyone else in that department. The truth is what you need in every department is a black sheep, somebody of whom you think, "This could be dangerous, because that is where the catalyst is." There is nothing better for self-growth than somebody challenging your own viewpoint.'

When I look at my personal catalyst moments, they have usually happened with people who are not like me. My assistant head at Grange was an extraordinary man. When we first met I thought he and I were going to be a match made in hell. He was ordered, organized, always logical, very sceptical. My worst nightmare. But he brought the best out in me, and I brought the best out in him.

You need the courage to trust yourself in the company of people who you think you are not going to have anything in common with. Our social conditioning makes us tend to hang out

Change

with people from the same context, because that is safe. But I urge people to invest in time beyond their own organizations, beyond their own line of work or business and to spend time meeting people who, on the surface, appear to have nothing to offer them.

Too often, I have come across people who make up their minds within seconds whether a conversation is of any use to them; who see no immediate, quantifiable benefit and therefore do not return calls or emails.

That is not to dismiss the value of traditional networking, often characterized as a mountain of embossed business cards spilling out into the darkest recesses of our faux leather document wallets. These days, of course, it also means LinkedIn or Facebook and the digital phenomenon that is friend-number envy. These things can be a force for good, but we frequently sterilize our lives by creating silos around us and our experiences.

A few years ago CNN invited me to participate in a think tank in London, bringing together people

Share

from diverse sectors: digital experts, TV producers, content developers, finance specialists, marketing directors, as well as people working with young people within and outside formal education. We had been brought together by a senior executive of CNN's parent company, Turner, to explore how CNN could produce a new service aimed at using its reach to bring young people around the world together to solve problems of mutual interest – providing clean water for a small village community in Burundi, say.

We spent two days and evenings together. Meeting so many people from such different backgrounds was inspirational. We worked up some concepts. But I would never have been invited to attend had it not been for a chance meeting a few months earlier, when the London Business Forum asked me to run a session on the future of education, and that Turner senior executive was in the audience. The new network had arisen because of an earlier connection – and so the ripples increase.

Change

To go out and talk, to connect, to communicate, requires a certain level of courage. Too many of us create social and professional boundaries that give us a set of justifiable reasons never to stray beyond the town limits or even our whitewashed picket fence. For most of us, if we do network, we do so within the closed loops of specific business sectors, school gates, social clubs or economic strata. Even the proficient corporate networkers make short-term judgements about the value of a new contact; choosing to bin or build within minutes of a handshake or smile. It is more than just a sad indictment of modern society that if something or someone doesn't fit into our immediate context they are very rapidly deemed to be of no value.

For the vast majority of my time as an educator, I associated with teachers: I married one, my children's godparents are teachers, my professional development was shared with them, I even went on holiday with them. Don't get me wrong, it was great: sociable, informative and comfortable. I learned a lot and gained many personal benefits,

Share

but it was only when I left education and became a freelance worker that I truly marvelled at the opportunities beyond the corral, meeting a diversity of people in a range of different settings, witnessing new scenarios, contexts and narratives that pushed and provoked me; stimulating my thinking and experience.

*Relationships are worth investing in and the best of those do not carry a quick win.*

Relationships are worth investing in and the best of those do not carry a quick win. In fact, they often seem to have no related use at all. Many politicians could learn from this: they are creatures of the short-term network, of the 'instant win'. I have so often seen them size people up in a handshake and dismiss them with their eyes, while I know that those people have so much to offer, to challenge and to provoke.

Edwin H. Land, one of the founders of the Polaroid Corporation, described politeness as 'the poison of collaboration'. As he explained, 'When collaborating with others, it is tempting to say that

Change

you like something, or that you think something is good, just to be polite. In reality, this does not advance the project or the idea being collaborated on. Any collaborative project should reflect the will of all those involved. By holding in what you really think, for the sake of avoiding hurting someone else's feelings, you destroy the opportunity for honest communication in a collaborative environment.'

At Grange School our staff was populated with headstrong, experienced and confident people. When we appointed, we selected people who would challenge and speak their minds too. Before I arrived, I had been warned that the staff there were difficult to manage and that some were detrimental to the future success of the school. They were certainly not a harmonious bunch, but they were passionate, with a profound sense of what they wanted for the school and the children. Many had been badly managed by external advisors and former heads: the instinct had been to control and to create uniformity through the imposition of

Share

*Some of the most dynamic moments came when we worked through clashes in personality, ideals and thinking.*

strategy and systems, rather than through collaboration.

Those same staff members, though, were the ones who created the school we became because of our commitment to collaboration and the power of collective thinking. It certainly was not easy, and at times there were arguments, conflict and uncomfortable moments, but they were part of the excitement that enriched and drove the process. Some of the most dynamic moments came when we worked through clashes in personality, ideals and thinking. The results were profound and on personal levels created deep relationships and trust that will last a lifetime.

Many of the most creative people I have encountered have had stories to tell about how they felt ostracized within and even forced out

Change

of organizations because they were considered to be trouble-makers. They said they became so after developing negative feelings towards their colleagues and managers but had not started out that way: they were keen, passionate people who were desperate to have their voices heard and to explore real opportunities for change.

By being aware of the signs of anxiety and creeping fear that will often result in resistance to change, you can recognize and act against them.

The signs of resistance to new experiences can be summed up as:

- general apprehension/anxiety when something new is suggested;
- bodily sensations of tension/rigidity when in a novel situation;
- attempts to self-medicate high levels of arousal/ anxiety with drugs/alcohol;
- tendency to complain along the way during new activities/experiences;
- choosing to focus on the negatives of the new experience, rather than the positives.

Share

When I first discovered this list, I started to realize that a number of colleagues, whom I had in the past written off as blockers, as bad employees with no skill or passion, were essentially good people who, on the whole, wanted to do a good job, but who were suffering from a high level of 'change anxiety'. If we write these people off too readily, which can often happen in times of high pressure, we are not only risking the morale of the wider team but we could be limiting the talent pool. The risk-averse person, managed correctly, may be the catalyst for the next great idea.

If we are to build momentum for change we must invest emotionally in the people as well as the vision. At times that can be hard but for me it is one of the signs of the truly great change leader.

Change

# Challenge for Change #6

We have learned to live with risk assessment policies and strategies, but how powerful would it be if, as a team, you were able to establish a risk-taking policy? How would you coerce the reticent and nervous. What professional development opportunities would you put in place to harness the power of the people around you, rather than being limited by their psychological difficulty in coping with change?

My stepfather was the person who did it for me. If I said it was night, he would say it was day. As a teenager this used to drive me mental. We had blazing rows over dinner about the most ridiculous things. Of course, he knew exactly what he was doing. He was forcing me to challenge my own viewpoint, to truly analyse the way I thought and behaved. I think the reason I am now a good communicator comes from the fact that my

Share

stepfather would deliberately play provocateur and allow me to challenge my own thinking, to constantly have to reframe and justify my position, who I was.

What should happen through those processes is that you start to find, at different points and stages of your life, different kinds of like-minded people. When your convention is challenged, when your thinking is challenged, you need the flexibility to say, 'Well, actually I am quite attracted to this group over here, the group I have looked at and previously thought, *Hmmm*.'

We have to move away from polarization and conflict towards collaboration. The most productive conversations I have had in education have been with people who come from a directly contrary position. We tend, because of our desire to pigeon-hole all the time, to have likes and dislikes: 'I'm not going to get on with him, we have diametrically opposed philosophies, he doesn't understand . . .' You need to sit down and have a constructive conversation. You might never agree – and that's

Change

fine – but you can still hone a philosophy. It is most likely that you will learn more from that person than the one you agree with.

As Sir Ken Robinson says in his seminal book on creativity, *Out of Our Minds*, 'It is often said that education and training are the keys to the future. They are, but a key can be turned in two directions. Turn it one way and you lock resources away, even from those they belong to. Turn it the other way and you release resources and give people back themselves. To realize our true creative potential – in our organizations, in our schools and in our communities – we need to think differently about ourselves and to act differently towards each other.'

*The key is to ensure that everyone in an organization is given the opportunity to experience all the diverse roles.*

During his time as coach of both Ajax and the Netherlands national team in the 1970s, soccer coach Rinus Michels developed the philosophy of 'total football'. His belief was that in order for the team to function

Share

at the highest level and to mix both efficiency and creativity, every player – no matter what their designated position on the field, or their strengths and weaknesses – should learn to play in every other position. By doing this, he created a system that did not allow players to exist in their own comfort zones. It helped them empathize with their teammates, encouraged them to feel like active stakeholders in the overall tactical lens of the team and ultimately ensured that every player had the opportunity to contribute to the way the team evolved. In some ways, his coaching married perfectly the ideals of productivity and change.

The key here is to ensure that everyone in an organization is given the opportunity to experience all the diverse roles within the set-up so they then feel they have a powerful voice.

I recently ran a seminar at a large investment bank in London. I knew that politics was in play when the people attending the seminar walked in, some one hundred in total. The customer services team sat together on one side, marketing in the

Change

middle; at the back were the IT team, responsible for digital infrastructure and delivery. As I began the seminar it became clear that every time the customer services team nodded, the IT staff scowled, and vice versa. During the Q&A session at the end, the division was made more explicit, as I heard variations on the phrase 'It's all very well for them to say that, but they have no idea what *we* are dealing with' preface every comment.

I had observed a similar scenario at Grange School: infighting caused by ignorance, in turn created by a lack of understanding of the challenges and processes being dealt with by others. These destructive divides – between teachers working with the youngest children and those teaching the older kids, for example – threatened to rip the school apart. Staff would sit in separate groups and time their breaks to avoid coinciding with other teams. There was even a deliberate strategy of marking 'generously' in the lower-school tests, with resulting grade inflation, so that the upper unit would have to take remedial

Share

action to bring the children up to artificially high levels to avoid what would look like drastic underperformance. In revenge, the upper school-dominated leadership team would underfund the lower unit...

The only remedy was to create a holistic system flowing through the whole school, based on a fixed, jointly accountable vision. Firstly, we introduced job exchanges, so that every teacher had to teach in every year group. We also encouraged all support and non-teaching staff to do the same. I wanted everyone to appreciate the challenges and efforts of their colleagues and have contexts within which to have meaningful conversations outside the classroom.

We also worked on creating a steel core running from the early years upwards. I asked the team what we wanted our students to look like, as human beings, when they left us at the end of their journey through Grange, and having done that, asked the staff – in groups made up of members from different units – to determine the behaviours we

Change

would explicitly need to develop in the children to realize that vision.

Finally, we created mixed project teams, again across the year groups, to work up strategies responding to specific challenges such as 'How to develop a greater culture of enterprise in the students'. The results were truly transformative: the staff became one united team. It is no accident that at the same time our test results experienced dramatic improvement throughout the school, this time without the need for artificial grade inflation.

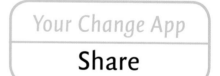

Your Change App

## Share

● There is no magic formula; no right or wrong way to build networks: trust your gut instinct and be prepared to expect that for every golden connection there may well be half a dozen that lead nowhere.

Share

- Get out there, meet people, and when you do, ask questions about their world. You will learn so much.

- After learning about other people's experiences, view their experiences through the lens of your own role. How can you apply what you have learned to your own context?

- Make an effort to get to know the people you are threatened by or who you know may be the polar opposite to you. We can learn more from the objective and constructive understanding of those we disagree with. Sometimes we are too quick to write them off. The more effort you make to understand others, the better you will know yourself and why you act the way you do.

Change

# DEVELOP

---

'To make change happen, you need
to rediscover the skills and tools that
so many of us have forgotten.'

# Change

We are born as creatures of change, of creativity and curiosity. Somewhere along the way we lose many of the skills and behaviours that allowed us to accelerate at such a phenomenal rate as youngsters. If we could recapture those feelings and that extraordinary raft of competencies we would be so much better equipped to deal with the world we now inhabit.

Remember that list of the ten common traits of truly great people: Focus, Preparedness, Conviction, Perseverance, Creativity, Curiosity, Resilience, Risk-taking, Independence and A sense of higher purpose. With the exception of a couple of those traits, the list would describe the behaviour of a young child.

How many of these traits are ever highlighted to us when we are young or explicitly nurtured as we develop? Yet we assume that as adults, as employers and as employees, we will automatically possess these qualities and use them when appropriate. I would like to explore the first five of them in ways that hold particular resonance for me, but ask you to review them in your own way, personally and professionally, and to consider how you can develop awareness of them and their deployment in others.

## Focus

As young children we are focused on the right now, the immediacy of our lives. As we grow older and our experiences enlarge we start to see, feel and think about more. We swim harder and faster just to feel that we can keep afloat and find less and less time to come up for air; we become obsessed

Develop

with not drowning, rather than learning to water-ski next.

Do many of us focus on the wrong things? As we develop, most people tend to focus on the things that they *can't* do rather than the things that they could do, or would like to do, and – often because of our lack of confidence to focus upwards and beyond – we will find reasons not to lift our heads above the parapet.

I have a friend for whom I have enormous respect, both professional and personal, but he has one major fault, which has led to his experiencing stress-related problems. As a school leader he is passionate about his job, his colleagues and the children in his care. When I first met him he was a dynamic thinker, happy to promote innovation and take calculated risks. However, as the pressures of his job intensified he found it harder and harder to focus outwards and project into the future.

He has become what I call a 'reactive' leader, responding to existing issues but also trying to control every factor within his own realm in order

Change

to avoid conflict or the possibility of future challenge. He is one of the kindest people I know and, as a result, he tries to keep everyone happy, which is of course impossible when you lead a large, complex team. I have watched him become paranoid about the most simple issues. He is so worried about his condition worsening that he has found himself trapped in a vicious circle of reactive actions which has left him unable to lead his organization forward.

I was recently on a trip to Australia, where I heard Walter Mikac from Tasmania tell his story at a conference. Until 28 April 1996, Walter, a pharmacist by trade, had lived a 'normal' life, happily married with two daughters aged six and three. One day his wife had taken their children to Port Arthur to meet friends. Shortly after lunchtime, they became three of the thirty-five innocent people killed by Martin Bryant in an unprovoked massacre. At the conference, Walter said that in his darkest moments – his entire family having been wiped out – he could see no point in

Develop

existing any longer. But he wrote a very personal letter to the then prime minister, John Howard, explaining his own feelings about the gun laws in the country at the time. John Howard invited Walter to meet him and discuss the issue further. Walter discovered his focus; he has since gone on to raise public support for gun law reform and to co-found a foundation in his daughters' memory providing support for children who are the victims of violent crime.

## Preparedness

Abraham Lincoln once said, 'When I am getting ready to reason with a man, I spend one-third of my time thinking about myself and what I am going to say and two-thirds about him and what he is going to say.' I have always used this quote as a mantra for leading people, if for no other reason than it would help me build a personal security around difficult meetings or conversations.

Too much of what we do and experience feels like we are simply running to keep up. That is how change feels for most people because, so often, it is a reactive process. You can't indulge in 'blue sky thinking' when the clouds are thundering and the rain is torrential; all you can do is put up an umbrella and run for cover until the whole thing passes over.

In one of the most well-known studies on creative visualization in sports, Russian scientists compared four groups of Olympic athletes in terms of their training schedules: Group 1: 100 per cent physical training; Group 2: 75 per cent physical training with 25 per cent mental training; Group 3: 50 per cent physical training with 50 per cent mental training; Group 4: 25 per cent physical training with 75 per cent mental training.

Amazingly, Group 4, with 75 per cent of their time devoted to mental training, performed the best. I have always used visualization techniques

You can't indulge in 'blue sky thinking' when the clouds are thundering and the rain is torrential.

Develop

to inspire students and realized that it was also a crucial lever in my leadership of others and my default way of rationalizing hard personal times and situations.

I first came across this technique as a student. I was part of a group exploring the writing of fiction; our lecturer used 'guided fantasy' as a stimulus. He would get us to relax, close our eyes and describe various scenarios to us, for example: 'Imagine you are on a dark lane late at night. What can you hear, see, smell? It has been raining, you are walking towards an old house . . .' This was a powerful technique for overcoming writer's block. I use a similar technique for widening experiences and developing aspiration.

Rafael Nadal often talks about finally knowing he could beat Roger Federer on grass at Wimbledon because for six months before the potential second final between them he had played every point in his head, so that when he was on Centre Court on Finals Day, he had already been there.

For any unfamiliar scenario that you face, where

Change

the uncertainty and anxiety of change may feature, visualization can be a valuable preparatory tool. As with play, simulation and visualization are processes we develop in childhood and use extensively as we learn and make sense of the world around us, but they are things we grow out of as we increase our dependency on others to protect us.

I have frequently used visualization in both my personal and professional life. As a head teacher, visualization was useful in unexpected circumstances. One parent had been throwing her weight around, swearing at and threatening members of staff whenever she had not got what she wanted for her child. We were proud of our open-door policy but with this particular mother, the time came to draw a line, as she had been ranting and raving in classrooms full of children.

I called her in, expecting that she would not show up. Nonetheless I played out two or three scenarios so that at the appointed time I would not be dominated by her behaviour or personality. She did turn up and, as I had anticipated, she was on the

Develop

attack from the outset, but I was able to deal with her and achieve the outcome I wanted. Remarkably, she even thanked me for my time, and – something she had never done before – apologized for her behaviour.

In a particularly tense lead-up to a speech, when I know I will be out of my comfort zone, I tend to visualize how I will feel afterwards. For example if I am driving into London to speak to a financial organization – and those are often the scariest things for me because I think they are probably about as far removed from my life as any group can be – what I tend to do is visualize the drive home. On the way I will be feeling tense, but thinking that three hours later I will be back in the car with a particular piece of music on, knowing I have done a good job, that the audience has been won

*When you are about to do something you feel threatened by, challenged by, it is really important to see yourself succeeding at the other end of it.*

Change

over and I can start thinking about the weekend. When you are about to do something you feel threatened by, challenged by, it is really important to see yourself succeeding at the other end of it.

## Conviction

When I was leading Grange School through some huge changes, I realized that the key to implementing those changes successfully was to convince the most influential members of staff of my sincerity and passion. On the day I left, I wanted to take time to thank the man who became my greatest advocate, my assistant head, Les, who on arrival I had thought would fight me all the way. I asked him why he had so quickly thrown his weight behind my leadership. His response was simple. 'Richard,' he said, 'the day I met you and you spoke to me about this school by talking about the children first, I knew that we came from the same place and I knew that, even if I thought that some of what you wanted to do was crazy, it was always based on what you thought would be right for them.' Even if

Develop

what we want to do or change is based on cold, hard logic, we must find ways to lead the communication of it from the heart.

In his book *Ronald Reagan: The Power of Conviction and the Success of His Presidency*, Peter J. Wallison, a former White House Counsel, asserts that Reagan took office with a fully developed public philosophy and strategy for governing that was unique among modern presidents. 'I am not a great man,' Reagan once said, 'just committed to great ideas.'

Marketing experts will often advise companies in the twenty-first century that the best way to demonstrate the conviction, commitment and quality with which they want to be associated is to find endorsement, which in turn conveys confidence and trust. Your conviction is not best translated to others by shouting or railroading but by gathering support through personal contact and interaction.

Many people are happy to be led if they find someone who encapsulates their own desires and beliefs, and does so with conviction. Children are experts in the detection of insincerity. They

Change

know if a teacher does not care for them as an individual; equally they can sense when a teacher is not passionate about what they are teaching. As a child, it was not so much the subject I loved; most often it was the teacher, like my science teacher, Mr Turnbull. I had struggled with the subject previously, but he was passionate about his subject, and he turned my results around. That was sometimes just by stopping me in a corridor and asking me about my drama activities, which he knew I was fascinated by. He took an interest in me as a person, not just a name on his register, and he hooked me into his own interests. He was authentic, a man of real conviction. It is an attitude I have tried to use ever since.

*Even if what we want to do or change is based on cold, hard logic, we must find ways to lead the communication of it from the heart.*

## Perseverance

I have battled weight gain for most of my life, not because I have a thyroid problem but because

Develop

I love food and loathe exercise, hence the resulting body mass situation. It is only in the last few years when I have bitten the bullet, amended my diet and started exercising regularly that I have started to see results. I had to stick at it, though, as it took months for my metabolism to click into the new regime and it was only by working with a personal trainer that I kept going.

Change is not a fast-food meal. When you are starting to shift an entire culture it cannot be achieved overnight with a supersized milk shake; it needs to be nurtured, developed and stuck to.

Our greatest problem is that most of us are conditioned from an early age not to persevere. As parents our instincts to nurture and protect our children from distress mean that we will often step in and help them too soon, from learning to read to fastening their coats. This is exacerbated in our adult lives by the incredible pressure we put ourselves under and the lightning pace at which we live.

As a supporter of Arsenal Football Club, I know

Change

the meaning of extraordinary resilience. I was born an Arsenal fan; my father and grandfather had supported the club all their lives. Unfortunately for me, my arrival as a supporter happened to coincide with a disappointing period for the club. Luckily, supporters tend to be a resilient bunch, going to matches week after week, always believing that the sun would shine tomorrow.

Resilience is born out of such beliefs. Refugees will endure the most horrifying journeys and risks in order to survive and find a better future. My own family did so when they fled Nazi Europe. To nurture resilience you must want something badly enough to endure setbacks and adversity, barriers and sometimes conflict while still finding a route through.

Develop

## Creativity

Sir Ken Robinson has described creativity as 'imaginative processes with outcomes that are original and of value'. His definition elegantly articulates the difference between imagination and the creative process. I have heard people state that creativity is a luxury that cannot be afforded in hard times. And I have listened to education commentators pass off creativity as something that gets in the way of standards and learning. What is clear is that creativity must not merely produce valuable outcomes but must itself be a process that is valued and encouraged.

Creativity is not a luxury item, the preserve of the safe and secure. It is the critical element in the development of an organic, actively changing culture. We must challenge ourselves harder to question how people's imaginations are encouraged and their ideas heard, no matter what their position or rank.

# Change

# Challenge for Change #7

How do we actively develop in people the ability to utilize their creativity and curiosity on a daily basis: to question, to challenge, to research, hypothesize and trial; to fail, to analyse, to evolve, refine, interrogate and share?

Develop

I have a hero. There are many people I admire and respect and some I aspire to be like, but I have only one real hero. It may surprise you because he is neither famous nor publicly admired.

He was a young man I met on my first day as a primary school teacher. His name was Gary, he was nearly ten years old and he was a pupil in my first 'proper' class. After my appointment to the job, I excitedly studied the names and backgrounds of that first group of children; I spent the summer reading every word about them, interrogating their previous teachers about their academic abilities, their personalities, their interests.

Gary, I was told, was a lovely lad who, because of a multitude of disadvantages including dyspraxia, dyslexia and dyscalculia, would never thrive academically. Our job was to make sure that he would 'have enough to get by'. It only took me a week to realize that Gary was someone special; very special. We did what a lot of schools do at the start of a new year to bind the community together – we held a charity week. The director of a charity that

Change

was funding a school and orphanage in Romania would talk to the children in an upcoming assembly, and we would spend the week raising money for the same cause.

One of the week's events was a 'non-uniform day', when the students would donate a few pence and in return be able to wear their own clothes to school. The children duly arrived dressed in their most fashionable attire and we collected the coins they had brought in. Gary, however, brought his money box containing his entire fortune – the best part of £100 – insisting that we took the lot. Clearly we couldn't accept, but Gary was adamant. I decided to phone his mother.

She had been expecting my call and urged me to take the money. She and Gary had spoken about it for hours the previous night. Gary had been saving for a bicycle, and had put aside his pocket money and some earnings from odd jobs in order to save up for it, but when he heard about the plight of the Romanian orphans he had changed his mind, saying to his mother that he would never be able

Develop

to enjoy the bike knowing where the money could have gone.

We accepted Gary's donation.

I was choked up and in awe of this boy and his selfless instincts. Throughout the short time he spent with me I was constantly inspired by his humanity and empathy. I lost touch with Gary a year later when he moved to secondary school but I never forgot him and often wondered what had become of him. Seventeen years later, I found out. A quirk of fate put us in touch and we met for coffee. The ten-year-old lad I remembered was now a man pushing thirty, which made me feel very old indeed. As we sat and sipped our frothy coffee, I asked him to talk me through the years since he left our primary school.

He started with a look of disappointment; he told me that he had really struggled at his senior school, failing to get any exam passes of value, and that he had left school at sixteen as a result. He had always been passionate about sport and had decided to try his hand at a career in the leisure

Change

industry, so he applied to the local college for a place on a sports management course. Sadly, he was turned down; apparently, having read his application form, the applications board decided that he wouldn't be able to cope with the academic rigour of the course. It would have been so easy for him to give up at this point, to project blame for the failure on anything, anybody, and to resign himself to the fate that had been defined by his own shortcomings.

But he didn't. Instead, he demonstrated his credentials as a risk-taker by deciding to apply for the same course at another college, but this time personally taking his application form to the admissions office bright and early one Monday morning and demanding to meet the admissions tutor. He was turned away, told to follow procedures and to post the form. He didn't, and returned to the office on Tuesday, Wednesday and Thursday. By the Friday, the office team were so sick of him that they arranged a meeting for him with the elusive tutor. He got a place on the course and

Develop

after two years graduated top of his class. Gary was not done yet, though; those two years had helped him focus and he now had a clear idea of what he wanted to do.

He had seen an opportunity, a gap in a market; he had also realized that his future lay in working for himself. He was fiercely protective of his own independence and had from an early age been taught that, as he puts it, 'the only person responsible for you, is you'. He realized he needed to finish his training and found an appropriate course in London, which ran only at weekends; it was a year long and required private funding. So this young man worked during the week to fund the last part of his education, his train fares and his accommodation in the capital.

As he spoke I beamed with pride. I was dying to know: what did he do afterwards, what was the gap in the market? He had set up his own business as a personal trainer for people who had physical and mental disabilities, a business he still runs today with a passion and commitment that is

Change

contagious. He allows himself one month off a year in December, but does not spend his downtime on a beach. He devotes his spare time to visiting a particular village in the developing world, offering his services for free. I am not sure that I have ever met anyone quite like Gary; at the age of ten he was special, as an adult he is inspirational.

I have often thought about Gary's journey and shared it with others, trying to work out what sets him apart. It is undeniable that he has all of the traits of greatness, but the one that defines and drives him is the one I think is the rarest trait of all: a powerful sense of higher purpose.

When we explore greatness we tend to look at individuals and their personal journeys as it appears far easier to identify their narrative. These people

Develop

also tend to stand out and provide inspiration for the rest of us.

If we are to successfully lead change and drive it personally and professionally, then we must develop a culture of vision with clear goals that give momentum to that vision. Goals cannot be imposed, they must be owned by the person who is working towards them. That is why Gary was so successful. He developed a clear sense of purpose, married it to his passion, trusted his instincts and then developed a single-mindedness which has defined his life.

Change

- It is not only method actors who need to search for motivation and challenge themselves to find it. Aim to find a sense of purpose, something that matters enough to you or those you are trying to involve to sustain the commitment.

- Develop the ability to assess yourself and to interrogate your own thinking and behaviour on a regular basis.

- Think about how you can move forward and what the future could look like, rather than only dealing with what comes your way.

- Ask yourself how you can enable your own journey from focus to resilience.

- Provide opportunities for people to step outside their daily routine. How can you give them

Develop

additional stimulus to reflect on and move forward from difficult situations and experiences?

● Find your own 'Gary', a personal hero whose journey has inspired you. When times get tough, ask what they would do in the same circumstances.

Change

# CHOOSE

---

'Be prepared to take the plunge –
and find somebody to help give
you a timely push.'

# Change

Change can present itself just when you least expect it. I was loving my life as the head of Grange School, thrilled and absorbed by what we were achieving there. Because the achievements of the school had started to gain quite a reputation in educational circles, I was asked to present a seminar at a conference for head teachers in the Lake District. The keynote opening speech was being given by somebody I had not then heard of called Ken Robinson, and as I had some time to spare before my workshop I grabbed a seat at the back of the auditorium to listen to his talk.

Ken Robinson had been very prominent in arts education, and in 1998 had been commissioned by Education Secretary David Blunkett to chair a committee investigating the creative and cultural development of young people through education. The committee's report, published as *All Our Futures*, offered strategies for the development of a more creative education system to meet the needs of a creative industry-driven economy. He was now Sir Ken Robinson, a guru of creativity and human capacity, a heavy-hitter.

As I sat listening to his address my mouth hit the floor, because Ken was articulating everything I had lived and breathed throughout my teaching career, especially when he was talking about developing people, not systems; about discovering what made people unique and allowing them to follow a path that was rich in context, rich in experience and, most importantly, was relevant.

I remember feeling emotional, thinking, *Oh my God, I am not crazy, I am not the only one who believes this.* I then went off to start my workshop. The first

Choose

few people came in, and I was quite intimidated because I wasn't used to public speaking. Just as I was about to start, a head popped around the door. It was Ken Robinson. 'Do you mind if I sit in? I've read the summaries of the workshops and this sounds quite interesting.' He came in, I did the workshop, and everyone left except for him. He stayed at the back, and I was terrified. Had I said something to offend him?

Ken came up to me: 'I have never actually come across anyone putting into practice to the depth that you have what I have been so passionate about. Can we have dinner?' And that dinner went on till four in the morning: I remember talking too much, too loudly and with far too much gusto.

Luckily Ken saw my verbal assault as proof of my passion and enthusiasm. (One of his great strengths is his ability to see the best in everyone.) He was a researcher, an academic, and although he had worked in many different settings he had never met a school leader who had lived out his beliefs. I was coming from the practical end, seeking to

# Change

understand why what we had done at Grange had worked, and now meeting somebody from the other end who had been developing theories all his life.

Ken became a mentor to me. Despite living on the other side of the world, he was always there to support me via email, text or telephone, and whenever he came back to the UK he would always make time for dinner. He encouraged me to consider other career possibilities: 'Richard, what you do and the way you talk has huge potential. You have got something really important to say to people not just in education but beyond.'

Fast forward three years. Ken and I met in the restaurant of a hotel just off the M1 near Leicester to catch up. The food was good quality, business-hotel fare: steak, fries, a side salad and a small glass of Shiraz. I had been excited about the meal as an opportunity to spend a whole evening with a man who was now not just a mentor, but a friend, a chance to share, to laugh and to reinforce beliefs and vision.

Choose

By now it was clear that my journey at Grange School was coming to an end and I was looking towards the future. I knew my experience had changed me and as a result of the school's success, I had begun to inhabit worlds outside the classroom, worlds that I was stimulated by. Ken knew this; in fact, he had been instrumental in designing the rocket and providing the fuel. I had already been given the opportunity to work with governments and speak at international events. I had started to meet inspirational thinkers and doers. I was wondering if I could possibly make a living talking to companies and organizations about my experiences, my passion and my convictions.

Over dinner I was playing through the conversations I had had with various friends and colleagues, with my wife and family. In many ways, I was very lucky indeed; I had a great job that I was good at, a stable salary and a cast-iron pension plan. There was no imperative to leave, no unavoidable decisions or moments of crisis that can so often lead people into enforced change. I had options, the most sensible

# Change

of which would have been to stay in the job I loved with the people I trusted and cared about.

However, I wanted to explore these new worlds, the opportunities that were opening up in front of me. I am a change agent by nature, always looking to develop, adapt and innovate.

I knew that Grange School had got to a point where it really didn't need me. I knew the school was fine, there was a legacy in place. That was important to me: I didn't want to leave and for everything to stop. I felt I could be best placed outside the system in order to provoke and challenge the status quo on a large scale with the weight of experience behind me. More importantly, I knew that if I stayed at the school I would start to instigate change, sometimes selfishly, in order to satisfy my own need for it, rather than for the good of the students and the community.

I was beginning to feel constrained by the day-to-day delivery of service and instinctively wanted both to have the time and space to push my thinking further, and to collaborate with people

Choose

outside the education sector. I needed a new challenge. And I was ready for this adventure.

It was a tense time, though, and I was guilty of doing what many of us do at similar crunch points: I found as many reasons as I could for not changing my job: genuine reasons such as financial security, that cast-iron pension, stability, family responsibility. But there was a nagging voice in the back of my head that said, *What if? What could happen, where could you go, what else could you achieve?*

*I was ready for this adventure.*

I asked Ken how he had known that the time was right for him to change his life and follow his dream, his passion. He had left a safe, secure post as a professor at a top university and gone on to become one of the world's most sought-after speakers, writers and broadcasters. On reflection, I'm not sure that he fully answered the question there, in that hotel, but he did fire the question back at me: 'I believe in you, the people you love believe in you and you have the talent to do this! What's really stopping you?' He went on, 'Trust

Change

me, I wouldn't encourage you if I didn't think this would work out. In years to come, when we meet for dinner and you have made a success of your new life, you'll wonder why you waited so long.' Then he finished with a flourish. 'Jump in,' he said. 'The water's lovely.'

Ken's encouragement and advice were critical in helping me make that decision. He understood me and what made me tick, he had experience in areas I was passionate about, but enough distance to be objective in his judgements.

That conversation changed my life. I arrived home about one in the morning, so wired that I wrote my resignation letter to the Grange's board of governors. That night I jumped and mentally prepared to hit the water.

Choose

# Challenge for Change #8

Can you find the confidence to respond to your own needs and instincts? To help you refine your focus, who is the right person to help you by acting as your sounding board, someone who you can be honest with, and who can be honest with you, who can share your thinking and feelings without the need to censor them?

The decision I took was the craziest thing anyone in a good public sector job would do: to chuck in my job and my pension to become self-employed and enter the speaking market with no guarantee of work or income. It was nuts. But once I had written the letter to the school governors I felt a massive weight had been lifted. I was euphoric. The fear only started to click in as I got closer to the day I finally left teaching. I had and I hadn't realized the depth of affection I had for the school, for the people I was working with, particularly

Change

for the children, and this was mixed with the apprehension of looking at my diary and knowing I didn't have a monthly income any more.

As the day of my departure loomed I remembered a visit I had made a little while earlier to a freelance education consultant, who had also been a head and had given up his headship a few years before. We were working on the design of some training programmes. He lived in Hampshire; I drove down and turned up at his house at half past eleven one autumn morning. He opened the door, and he had an apron on. 'I'm making us some soup for lunch,' he said. It was a work day. And for my entire career I had been used to being in school five days a week, every day of the school year. Here he was calmly making soup...

We had lunch – the soup was delicious – and cracked on for a couple of hours, before he said, 'I hope you don't mind, Richard. I've got to finish at three because I have promised my boys that I will pick them up so we can choose some fireworks for Bonfire Night together.' I told him, 'I have got

Choose

to be honest, I am really attracted to your lifestyle. I start work at 7.15 in the morning, I get home at eight, nine o'clock at night, completely knackered.' 'Yes,' he said, 'I've been through that. I just decided one day I wanted to spend more time thinking and doing and being in more control of my life. I have done my time.'

Waking up on the first morning after I had left Grange School, the shirt that had been signed by all the children and the staff was next to the bed along with a stack of leaving cards. I had fallen asleep reading them, a tear in my eye, emotionally wrung out after leaving the people I had worked with, cried and laughed with through some pretty extraordinary times. That night I dreamt of the children I had taught over the years, the lives that I had touched and the lives that had so profoundly touched me. But with the dawn came the dawning that after all those amazing years, it was now me; I was on my own and, if I'm honest, on that cold January morning as my wife headed off to work and my children to school, I rather liked it.

# Change

*I felt free because suddenly the only person*
*I was responsible for professionally was me.*

And what was the very first thing I did on my very first day when I had given up my headship? I made soup. In a way it was a symbol of a new freedom. The act of making soup meant nothing to anybody else, but as I was cooking I was smiling like a Cheshire cat. And that afternoon I went to pick my kids up from school.

That day I felt truly free. I felt free because suddenly the only person I was responsible for professionally was me. That was hugely liberating after having spent all my life in a world which was about giving everything to other people.

It was the same sense of liberation that Ferran Adrià must have had when he made his decision to close down El Bulli. It led to an advancement in his own mindset and helped to crystallize his thinking and methods. It would have been very easy for him

Choose

to stay put, open a chain of similar restaurants, become a TV celebrity chef. Yet he took a calculated risk and jumped.

'Do you miss it? Do you ever want to go back?' These are the questions that I get asked more than any other, but they are also questions I ask myself every day of my new life. I didn't think about it in the first few weeks after leaving. I was so absorbed with the freedom: freedom from rules and responsibility for others. Most of my professional life had been spent in a school, a place full of people, always busy, usually noisy and mostly demanding.

I was also busy in those first few weeks, starting to try and build up a speaking programme, travelling, speaking, meeting new people and experiencing new things. In a way, I didn't have the time to dwell on what I'd left behind – until one terrible night in London.

I had been booked for my first after-dinner speech, with an audience of more than a thousand people at the Intercontinental Hotel on Park Lane. This was something I had been so looking forward

Change

to, a real 'if they could see me now' moment. I was going to be speaking in front of some global CEOs and employees at an international event, held to celebrate their industry . . .

I arrived at four in the afternoon for a speech scheduled for 10 p.m., and walked into the vast ballroom where the arrangements for the evening were well under way: huge screens, lights that wouldn't look out of place at a rock concert. Around the edge of the room, beyond the huge, round dinner tables decorated with elegant flower arrangements, the events team were setting up a bucking bronco, a giant Scalextric track and a candyfloss machine.

I was too naive for any alarm bells to start ringing. They didn't even tinkle, even when I was told by the organizers there was a free bar starting at 5 p.m. and that I was going to be on after The Mystical Zorbo, the magical mind-reader. I did check my brief: they wanted me to talk about the importance of self-esteem and personal image. They were insistent that that was exactly what

Choose

they wanted: 'Something thought-provoking and emotive,' they said.

By the time 10 p.m. arrived, Zorbo had guessed the colour of people's underwear – one woman, we discovered, wasn't wearing any – the bronco was bucking, the miniature racing cars flying around the magnetic track and people were sick on candyfloss and free booze; my time had come.

What happened next is almost too painful to relive. I stood in front of the celebratory crowd, many of whom were now indulging in the fairground distractions around the borders of the room, and I started to flick through my PowerPoint slides, talking earnestly about how people's feelings about themselves were often developed during their school days. I talked about my own obsession with my weight as an example, to which a chorus of 'Who's the fatboy on the stage?' broke out from the growing, informal choir. I was caught in the cross-hairs, not knowing what to do. My inexperience was being cruelly exposed. I wanted to walk off but was worried that might breach my contract. So I tried

Change

to ignore the idiots and spoke to the one table who were politely listening to me at the front of the room: the organizer and some of the organization's senior directors. It was the longest forty minutes of my life.

That night, back in my very glamorous room, I cried like a baby. My family was 150 miles away, it was late and I had bombed. I am not sure that I could ever remember feeling so alone. The next morning as I travelled back on the train, staring out of the window at the sheep and puddles, I realized just what I had left behind: my school, the children, my colleagues, and for the first time I realized how important they had all been to me on an emotional level. Those people, with whom I had shared so much, had been my inspiration, my support and my security. Change is not easy. I felt drained but decided to stick with it.

Choose

## NEW WORLDS

Not long afterwards I found myself standing in the home of Matt Goldman, one of the founders of The Blue Man Group, in the heart of New York's Soho, surrounded by a group of celebrated architects, designers, performers, social campaigners and business leaders. We had been gathered together by Ken Robinson, because as he had travelled the world, he had met a range of people he wanted to bring together, to mix up some ingredients and to see what cooked.

I had never visited New York before. Here I was in the coolest of loft apartments at an extraordinary gathering. Underneath the glamour and romance, I was terrified. In my own world, as an educator, I was supremely confident. I had led a school to global recognition and was comfortable talking to government ministers, heads of state and world leaders about that experience, but this was entirely different. I felt like a little boy again, on his first day at 'big' school. Worse, I felt like a fraud. There in

Change

front of me were people who were talented and successful in their fields, fields that grew a long way distant from my little meadow on the Nottingham/Derby border. I am sure that I am not the only one who feels that my experience and skill are worthy only in my own realm, in my case teaching and school leadership. On reflection, it was precisely why Ken had asked me to join this group. It would teach me a vital lesson.

As we sat down to dinner, we were asked to go around the table and explain who we were and what we did. Ken began. I was only half-listening, as I was too busy rehearsing what I was going to say. I did catch snippets, though: a former presidential advisor, a producer for *Oprah*, the co-founder of Conscious Capitalism. When it was my turn my mind went blank. There was a pause, then a silence. Everyone waited patiently. I thought I was heading back into my post-Zorbo hellhole.

Then Terri, Ken's wife, who could see my rabbit-in-the-headlights expression, stepped in to help. 'Richard, tell us about your amazing school.'

Choose

I did, people clapped and then started latching on to the generics and sharing how they had overcome similar issues concerning leadership and change, promoting innovation and personal growth. Within minutes I had forgotten that I was the former school teacher from a place that people had only heard of because it was a few miles from the home of Robin Hood and I was engrossed in conversations that enthralled, challenged and stimulated me in equal measure.

When I finally got to bed, all I could think of was my former school and how much better I could have been as its head if I had had that dinner conversation a few years earlier. I realized that night that I had a significant set of experiences to share with others but still so much to learn from people beyond my immediate networks.

Before New York I had believed that the issues I was juggling with were unique to education; listening to what the others at the dinner had to say, I realized how connected we all were. By understanding their different strategies and

Change

situations I was able to clarify my own actions and broaden my horizons. It showed how spending time in the company of apparently unconnected people could give a dramatic push to your thinking.

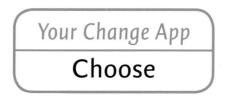

- Monitor yourself closely. Analyse your actions, motivations and instincts but don't pre-censor them based on what others expect.

- Then allow yourself to be selfish: recognize and respond to your own needs. This can be counter-intuitive, particularly for a leader in an organization.

- Find a mentor and open up yourself to meeting people from worlds beyond your own.

- When you are ready to jump, do it with conviction, gusto, an open mind and a brave heart.

Choose

- There will be times when things go wrong. Accept that and know that it is the most important time to separate out sentiment from your feelings. Tiger Woods once said that after hitting a bad shot, he would allow himself ten strides to rant about it internally. By the eleventh stride he would have parked his bad feeling and started looking forward to the next shot.

Change

# LEAD

'Our ability to change, to
lead change and to love change
is entirely dependent on the way
we behave and the conditions our
behaviour creates around us.'

# Change

As the world becomes smaller, new tools at our disposal allow us to become ever more connected, well informed and apparently in control of so many aspects of our lives, but an increasing number of people appear to live with a growing sense of disenfranchisement. Both personally and professionally, there is an escalating frustration in so many people that appears to come from a belief that as the world evolves and becomes more complex, so the locus of control is slipping away from the individual.

We see it in democratic politics, where the

electorate appears to be forfeiting its right to vote; in the UK in 1950 the percentage of eligible voters who exercised their right to vote in the general election was 84 per cent; by the 2010 elections the downward trend resulted in a figure of 65 per cent, with an alarming drop among younger voters.

A 2002 report into the lack of youth participation in local government found two primary reasons for it: a perception that there was little interest in their views, and a belief there was no point in voting because it was unlikely to bring about change.

Pamela Smith of Radboud University Nijmegen has observed that, 'people who perceived themselves as lacking power, suffered from an impaired ability to keep track of ever-changing information, to parse out irrelevant information, and to successfully plan ahead to achieve their goals'. The challenge stands that in order to love change, and therefore be able to lead it, we need to feel that we can control it and not be victims of it.

A few years ago I came across the work of Professor Henry Jenkins, formerly of MIT and

Lead

currently Provost Professor at the University of Southern California. He is one of the world's leading experts in new media technologies. For many years he has been talking about the skills required to be considered literate in a digital world. Many of these are appropriate far beyond the digital realm and hold real value for us all. They can have a profound impact on an individual's sense of control and well-being. In the following paragraphs I consider several of them.

## Play

Too many people see play only as something for children, a state that we leave behind with the carefree days of youth and blissful ignorance. Even as children, once we reach a certain age and stage, play is an activity for leisure time, something that must be earned as a result of good behaviour or hard work, a luxury item.

Play allows children to be 'in charge' instead of being told what to do and how to do it. It helps them explore and learn about the world they live in,

Change

builds their self-esteem and social skills, and gives them an opportunity to work out their feelings.

Play stimulates curiosity, creativity and innovation. The bottom line is that we *must* play more; play is the central reason that our learning is so profound and dynamic as toddlers and is, ironically, something we learn to devalue as we age. If we stop thinking of play as an idle pastime and treat it as something far more productive, it becomes a constructive part of our own mental journey and preparation for what comes next.

Psychiatrist Dr Stuart Brown, President of the US National Institute of Play, gave a popular TED speech in 2009 urging that adults should not set aside time to play. Rather we should infuse every moment of our lives with play. Organizations such as IBM, Deloitte & Touche, Google and Microsoft all use play as tools for motivation, development and staff satisfaction.

Lead

## Performance

No one set of conditions or parameters defines the criteria for optimal performance. This can be a real challenge in traditional management systems which assume that all people are motivated by the same things, are stimulated by the same experiences and work best under the same conditions.

Unfortunately our traditional education structures are again responsible for trying to standardize our behaviours and personal responses in the name of efficiency and mass development. A number of highly influential educational thinkers have for many years argued that to create life-long learners and people capable of sustained personal and professional development, children need to be made aware of their own value systems and under what conditions they learn best.

For example I am at my most productive when I am working to a deadline. I tend to be something of a big thinker and as a result I need the enforced structure of a fixed end point to produce something tangible; others thrive best in more open-ended

## Change

conditions. When I am writing I like to work by natural light, with a view, and music playing in the background. It helps me shut out the real world.

It is essential to treat everybody as an individual and respect their personal motivations and performance indicators. In short, standard-ized performance management will always have a limited impact and will constrain rather than maximize potential for growth, development and achievement and as a result, act against the empowerment principle.

## Visualization

For any unfamiliar scenario that you face, where the uncertainty and anxiety of change may feature, visualization can be a valuable preparatory tool.

As noted earlier, play, simulation and visualization are processes we develop in childhood and use extensively as we learn and make sense of the world around us, but grow out of as we increase our dependency on others to protect us.

Lead

The beauty of this process is that it remains a personal and private experience, even if you are in a room full of people doing the same thing. Some feel uncomfortable sharing it or admitting to others that they use it, but such techniques should become commonplace in any organization looking to establish a culture of change.

## Correct behaviour

As adults we take good behaviour for granted as a trait of maturity and experience, but I cannot be the only person who is sometimes astounded by the attitude of certain 'responsible adults' towards their peers. I have often come across teachers, for example, who will complain that their students rarely put up their hands, volunteer answers to questions or are prepared to engage in risky learning. These are the same teachers who, when asked to do the same thing at a training day, will deploy the same invisibility techniques as their slighted charges: gazing at their shoes, pretending to be deep in thought or suddenly finding

Change

something of urgent importance on the notes in front of them.

Too often we expect others to respond and behave in ways that we would not do ourselves. We expect people to suspend belief and behave in ways that they can see, through our own behaviour, are simply a construct: for example those managers who profess that they want to see their people 'seize the initiative' only to micro-manage their every move to ensure that their own backs are covered.

Lead

# Challenge for Change #9

Ask yourself three questions. First, how well do you know yourself, your grounding, your anticipated reaction to uncertainty and your abilities to manage those emotions? If you have a sound awareness you can use visualization and stimulation techniques to help build an emotionally familiar grounding on which to embark on a new challenge. Anticipating anxiety and pressure can give you a sense of control over them when you proceed for real. Secondly, how well do you know those people you are leading or encouraging through change, their levels of self-efficacy, their coping techniques, their abilities to overcome their own emotional barriers? And most importantly, how sympathetic and skilled are you in helping them to develop their personal awareness?

## Self-efficacy

Great educators know that their first task is to build self-esteem, confidence and a high degree of self-efficacy – the ability to complete tasks and achieve goals – in the children they teach; without it children will struggle with the concept of formal learning. Too many pupils go through education without that support and grow into adults whose self-efficacy has never been valued or nurtured. As a result they protect themselves by building walls of denial and isolation so they do not have to expose their weak underbellies. It is not that the person is incompetent, it's just that they aren't confident. Like all things precious, efficacy is easy to undermine and extremely hard to rebuild.

## Multitasking

Multitasking appears to have entered the realms of brain science in the 1990s as the fascination between human and artificial intelligence began to grow; it has developed almost mythical status like the Loch Ness Monster or the G-spot and been passed off as the unique skill of the young and of women. The psychiatrist and author Edward Hallowell is quoted as saying that multitasking is

Lead

a 'mythical activity in which people believe they can perform two or more tasks simultaneously as effectively as one'. There is a school of thought which argues that constant attempts to multitask and to be seen to operate that way can have a detrimental effect on our personal and professional performance.

In my professional life I have always had to control my own instinctive fascination with the new and different in order not to provoke panic and hysteria in those around me. In leadership I always needed a detail person, a grafter – some might say, a strong-handed minder – around me, to ensure that I stuck to one idea and saw it through.

Change is not the same as a stream of consciousness and successful change agents are not people who flit from one idea to another. Change requires focus and discipline and, most importantly, time. The key to success in an ever-changing environment is to evolve great peripheral vision that ensures that – like a bird pecking at seed – you keep looking up and around you to see what

Change

threats, and opportunities, are on the horizon. It's a balancing act.

The art of the multitasker is to be able to pursue a vision with vigour while always looking for the next stage in the narrative, the next chapter: the skill comes in how you connect the two and control the desire to move on ahead of time.

## Networking

The skill of a great networker is to process experiences to find common themes or threads, however tenuous, that may not be instantly usable but can be stored up for when the right moment arrives or is cultivated.

Social networking excites me when I see it used well. Twitter has unbelievable potential when used skilfully and with purpose, as do Facebook and LinkedIn. I am just not sure whether we have really begun to exploit the potential they offer as ways to push ourselves beyond what we already like or know. My favourite form of online networking is personal, intellectual networking or surfing; a couple of hours

Lead

*The key to success is to evolve great peripheral vision – keep looking up and around you to see what threats, and opportunities, are on the horizon.*

with a search engine, a starting theme for the search box and then away I go – organic exploration with no predefined end point.

This is the perfect metaphor for networking for change. We must make more time for abstract meetings, conversations and connections; we must be more relaxed about every interaction needing to be justified with an instant outcome.

If we are really to drive the principles of change to the heart of our culture, then we need to invest time and effort in laying the foundations. That requires focused approaches to the recruitment and development of managers, maybe even changing the profile of those we identify with potential, looking for deeper human characteristics rather than system thinkers.

Change

We also need to find and hone the tools within us, the emotional intelligence, the natural empathy needed to draw out these attributes in others.

*In too many settings we have identified the right approaches but have put them in the wrong hands.*

We can come up with a million strategies and tools but if we don't identify the right person to use them and implement them we are in trouble. I fear that in too many settings we have identified the right approaches but have put them in the wrong hands.

I have always measured how empowered people around me feel by their willingness to debate, discuss and negotiate. As a school leader, I loved it when members of staff or even children would walk into my office and start negotiating with me over strategies, systems or school rules: they would challenge my thinking with confidence and informed reason. In the early days some would apologize before making their point; I was really excited when they didn't feel the need.

Lead

The principle of empowering others is easy to project, but time-consuming and tough to master. It requires the confidence to expose emotions, securities and insecurities, it demands honesty and trust and the substantive and sustained investment of time, energy and belief; because the principle can only be put into practice if the culture is real enough to nurture it.

Change

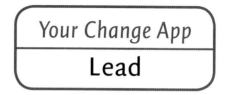

Your Change App

# Lead

● Change is a complex and highly personal concept. Even in a corporate environment it is the human reaction and capacity to embrace it that mean the difference between long-term success and failure. I have distilled six principles that I think define the key strategies that ensure a healthy and sustainable culture of change:

1. Lead by example, take risks and demonstrate that it's all right to fail.

2. Encourage the people around you to try new things and take risks. Provide guidelines with parameters and a means of measuring results. Stand ready to support them if they need assistance.

3. Encourage creativity and allow others the freedom to challenge authority and the status quo.

Lead

4. Do not discount new ideas.

5. Recognize and reward best efforts even if they fail.

6. Debrief and evaluate results. Identify things that worked well. Determine how things could be improved next time. Identify lessons learned.

# TRANSMIT

---

'If you have embraced the nature
of change and mastered the
process of change, then it should
happen imperceptibly, like the
daily growth of a child.'

# Change

As a teacher one of my favourite days in the school year was the last day before the summer break, not because of the holidays coming up, but because of the leavers' assembly. It was always a highly charged, emotional occasion, the one day in the year when I could stand back and reflect on legacy, on the students who had been taught in and nurtured by the school, on the way they had grown and developed.

One of my responsibilities as the head at Grange was to make the closing comments to the leavers. I would urge them never to stop wondering, dreaming and questioning, always to think like children. I would also tell them to look back as they walked out of the gates for the last time as pupils and to remember they would always be part of Grange, that they had helped make the school what it was.

But then I wanted them to turn and look down the road to where they were going and to what they would do next, to consider what mark they would make on the future. I asked them to carry on throughout the rest of their lives walking forward and challenging themselves to explore.

Although this message was obviously meant for children coming to the end of their early education, it holds a resonance for us all. The last time I gave that speech was my own last day at Grange. On that day I was giving myself the pep talk.

'Is it still the same though, Richard?' Every time I talk to educators about my work at Grange, or am interviewed about the school in the media, I am asked that question. 'Have they kept it going, does it still run the way you planned it?' Always they

Transmit

ask, 'Has it changed?' and my answer is always the same: 'I hope so . . .'

My task at Grange was to create a school that successfully prepared our students for their futures, futures that would be constantly shifting. I set out to create an organization capable of that organic challenge: to be able to self-reference, assess and evolve. For that to happen and for it to become habitual, we needed to develop the way of thinking into a way of life and then transmit it to the students.

Capacity for change can only accurately be measured through the legacy, the quality of the continued journey. A change culture that is mature, confident and resilient is one that requires little formal intervention or stimulation.

After I resigned as the head, I stayed away from the school for some time, deliberately, so that the new person in charge could develop the dynamic necessary in order to make their mark. I drove past the gates recently, and had a smile on my face. The physical landscape had changed: at the centre of the

Change

wonderful old buildings was a new market garden, a metaphor for growth and development. The school had continued to evolve.

There are times when change needs to be a focus, a highly conscious and driven process. But for too many people, in too many organizations, this is the default setting, not the exception. It should be the other way round. When programmes of change are imposed, led and followed it means that dependency cultures are never challenged. They are simply underlined and as a result, perversely, they can actually drain the capacity for change rather than promote it.

On a personal level, most people only think about change at a time of crisis: the loss of a job or the breakdown of a relationship. If we continue to relate to change in this way we can never win the race. It's as if we are giving Usain Bolt a two-second head start before the crack of the gun.

In the IT sector the word 'legacy' is used in the context of 'legacy systems', a term adopted to describe outdated technology: software, hardware, applications that an organization keeps running because it still, superficially, meets the users' needs but which beneath the surface is causing huge problems – software malfunction due to incompatibility, inefficiencies compared to new processes or systems and confusions and clashes with obsolete terminology or processes. Left too long and unchecked these systems can eat away at an organization's capability and in the worst cases crash entire networks. However, there are many reasons why organizations maintain legacy systems:

- The system works satisfactorily, and the owner sees no reason for changing it.
- The costs of redesigning or replacing the system are prohibitive because it is large, monolithic and/or complex.
- Retraining on a new system would be costly in lost time and money, compared to the anticipated appreciable benefits of replacing it (which may be zero).
- The system requires near-constant availability, so it cannot be taken out of service (an air

Change

traffic control system, for example), and the cost of designing a new system with a similar availability level is high.

- The way that the system works is not well understood, because the designers of the system have left the organization, and the system has either not been fully documented or documentation has been lost.
- The user expects that the system can easily be replaced when this becomes necessary.

NASA found itself stuck in precisely this dilemma and it was partly due to the legacy system around the space shuttle that it had to be retired from service in 2011. While many people, like NASA, realize and accept that economies of scale mean that wholesale replacement would be impossible, most look at the modern technology arena and wish that they had known then what progress has to offer now.

It is possible to create similar questions for other areas of organizational life or indeed personal change, for example:

- My life is settled, everything is comfortable;

Transmit

why rock the boat? The costs associated with changing my job, home and lifestyle are prohibitive because my finances and dependants create high levels of complexity.

- The process of starting again in a new field would take time, effort and possibly material cost ... and who says I'd benefit anyway?
- I have so many bills to pay, direct debits, mouths to feed; I cannot take time out to break the cycle.
- I have left it too long, become so stuck in my ways, I'm not sure I'd know where to begin.
- Despite all that, I reckon that if I really wanted to change I could at any time.

The answer is not to come up with excuses and prevarications but to change your mindset and lifestyle, which is a long-term commitment, not an easy flirtation. A sustainable change culture is a continuous and developing way of thinking.

As opposed to the IT definition, I prefer to define the word 'legacy' as something of value, to be cherished and nurtured. You cannot overlay an

Change

old legacy with a new one just because it has lost its relevance. The inaction and resentment that have developed as a result of initiative overload in workplaces – where new strategies have been introduced on top of existing systems and practice – have irrevocably damaged trust and positive thinking. It is vital that we recognize that emotionally as well as organizationally we cannot transform thinking and behaviour overnight.

One approach to continuous, incremental change is *kaizen*, a method and philosophy which originated in Japan. *Kaizen* translates to mean 'change (*kai*) for the good (*zen*)' and is based on the philosophical belief that everything can be improved. Some organizations look at a process and see that it's running fine; organizations that follow the principle of *kaizen* see a process that can be improved. This means that nothing is ever seen as a status quo – there are continuous efforts to improve which result in small, often imperceptible, changes over time. These incremental alterations accumulate to make a

Transmit

*Emotionally as well as organizationally we cannot transform thinking and behaviour overnight.*

substantial difference over the longer term, without having to go through any radical innovation. It can be a much gentler and employee-friendly way to institute the flexibility that becomes necessary as a business grows and adapts to its changing environment.

The *kaizen* philosophy was developed to improve manufacturing processes as an evolution of Taylorism and time-and-motion studies. You can use *kaizen* both at a personal level and for your whole team or organization.

Organizations that have adopted *kaizen* approaches have seen a number of benefits, including:

- People are more satisfied – they have a direct impact on the way things are done.
- Improved commitment – team members have a

Change

greater stake in their job and are more inclined to commit to doing it well.

- Reduced staff turnover – satisfied and engaged employees are less likely to leave.
- Improved problem solving – looking at processes from a solutions perspective allows employees to solve problems continuously.
- Improved teams – working together to solve problems helps build and strengthen existing teams.

At its heart, change is about very human traits: emotional, physical and personal. You can only generate a genuine legacy for change if you work hard to transform the behaviour of an organization's members and then the cultures within it, so for me a change legacy must begin and end with people, not systems, strategies or techniques.

A diet does not change a person's life, though it may have a short-term impact. I should know, I've tried hundreds, but I've seen them as processes with an end point (when I can drink alcohol

Transmit

and eat chocolate again). The reality is you can improve your fitness and body shape only through a long-term commitment to a change of lifestyle, and that, in turn, can be brought about only through a long-term change of behaviour and attitude.

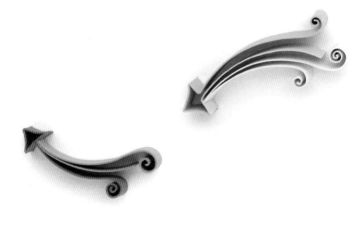

Change

# Challenge for Change #10

The legacy you leave is not going to be physical, easy to see, touch or describe; it will not necessarily be apparent in the form of strategic or systemic planning, because if you have led the right way and taken change to the heart of people's thinking and behaviour, then it will be the people you have touched and left behind who will, in their own way, be a testament to your legacy.

Acceptance of change will be evident in your behaviour and general approach to life and work. I do not mean that change will always be something to feel excited by. Uncertainty and the stress it can bring will always be a justifiable and real reaction to the elements of a less defined world. It will be your ability to keep your head above the parapet, to scan, radar-like, the scenarios around you and to anticipate new thinking, new trends and actions that will keep you on your toes.

Transmit

I recently heard the famous Spanish scientist, economist and broadcaster Eduard Punset urge an audience to trust their instincts more. What a liberating thing to say when for the most part we are urged and taught to trust evidence, proof and logic. The more I thought about it the more I agreed with him; so much of what I have achieved in my life has been as the result of following a hunch, an instinct, a feeling; I suppose I would describe myself as an action first, evidence second kind of person.

We need to ensure that we remain alert to the world and aware of our changing role in it. We must not over-complicate our reactions and response in an effort to justify ourselves. As Eduard Punset suggests, we must use curiosity and experimentation and take risks. We do not need a mystical sixth sense, but we do need to create the conditions that allow us to expand our horizons and our awareness of the world beyond our immediate contexts. We can only do that by committing to new experiences, contacts and opportunities.

Change

Instincts are a result of experiences and insights and can often be the moment at which two or more previously unconnected experiences join to form a pattern of understanding or thought. All people are born lucky, but as we develop, the ones who are seen to be so are the ones who are always on the look-out for an opportunity and then who have the courage to exploit it.

## OUTSIDE THE SYSTEM

I have a friend called John, who sometimes drives me to and from airports. By rights he should now be enjoying retirement, but the idea bores him. He has spent his life as a serial entrepreneur. Born in the north-east of England into a working-class family, school 'passed him by', but he was always interested in the mechanics of making money: trading, buying and selling. He always has a little deal on the go; a container of some diverse stock comes his way, he buys it, locates a market and shifts it on. He goes on instinct of what he thinks

*All people are born lucky, but as we develop, the ones who are seen to be so are the ones who are always on the look-out for an opportunity and then who have the courage to exploit it.*

will sell, how to sell it and where to sell it. He has a steely determination, extraordinary resilience, a love of life and an infectious enthusiasm.

Over time John has gathered like-minded people around him and they have created a consortium. They collaborate, share expertise, learn from one another and exploit each other's talents. It's a 'soft' consortium in that different people come together depending on the job, the challenge, the opportunity, but at the heart of it all is his vision, his drive. It wasn't until recently that I realized John was running a very twenty-first-century enterprise: fleet-footed, organic and as a result, incredibly responsive to trend and change.

John bypassed the traditional 'systems' of education and expectation, and as a result flows freely through a complex age with extraordinary

Change

success. He was never taught to look for the right answer or the safe passage. He was never told that only fixed routes would lead to successful outcomes. John is a 'life adventurer' who wakes up in the morning and, come rain or shine, knows that he can make it an interesting day. We need more Johns, and we cannot nurture them outside the system.

*We must each of us commit to living our lives to the fullest, pushing ourselves to find new experiences and opportunities.*

The mantra I developed for Grange School – 'Living, Learning, Laughing' – contains core beliefs that I think stand us all in good stead. If we are to find sustainable futures in an ever-changing world, we must each of us commit to living our lives to the fullest, pushing ourselves to find new experiences and opportunities. We must challenge our own thinking and behaviour constantly so that we don't suffer from complacency and, as a result, stop learning. If we become obsessed with controlling all the variables that spin around us, we will never

Transmit

feel happy. We must learn to relax and trust in ourselves more.

In my work as a speaker and consultant I try to pass on the benefits of my experiences and observations to create a new legacy, rippling out from any interaction I have: a seminar, a conference crowd, the readers of a book.

The only way I can judge that legacy is against the emails and informal feedback I receive. I am always gratified when someone tells me, 'I was on the verge of giving it up and you have reignited my passion and belief in change within the system.'

I recently ran a small round-table session at the London Business Forum. There were some people in the room from publishing, someone from the Criminal Courts of Justice and a couple of managers from the health sector. We had a really good session and everyone was very open, which was what I had hoped for: I was just the catalyst for people to open up, allow themselves to say the things they would never say in a meeting in their own environment. I wanted them to realize how connected they were

Change

to people from different backgrounds; they shared similar problems and issues around change and leadership.

Three months later I received an email from one of them, a woman who worked in the personnel department of the NHS. 'Dear Richard,' she wrote, 'About two weeks after your session, I was told I was being made redundant and put on gardening leave immediately. I just wanted you to know that, but I think I will be OK, particularly after you talked about re-connecting with your own passions and visions.'

I emailed her back and suggested a meeting. (I always feel intensely loyal to anybody who is prepared to connect with me.) When we met for a coffee, we had a one-to-one version of the seminar. She had been extremely frustrated by the often negative and unproductive attitudes displayed by her former colleagues and bosses. We talked about how she could turn her redundancy into something positive, and her frustrations into an opportunity for change.

Transmit

I said, 'Why don't you start blogging about it and getting your message out there?' So she began blogging and that in turn led to her setting up her own business consultancy specializing in the health sector, helping organizations uncover jarring and malfunctioning relationships and situations. When she contacted me to tell me she had launched the consultancy, she wrote: 'I realize that what you did during that session was awaken my awareness and understanding of things I had forgotten. I've been able to use it because now I am aware. It has changed my life.'

I often say to people, 'I cannot tell you how, I can't tell you what to do. All I can do is get you to think about how you empower yourself and then it's over to you.'

I can see the shape of my own journey. I started out working to make ends meet when I left school. I had the opportunities to develop my skills and hone a career, which I did as an educator. I instinctively began to push my own boundaries and explore the innovation in education and finally I jumped

Change

fully into a more organic, innovative stage, the life I lead now.

It is a life I love for its freedom of choice and movement, its adventure and constant stimulation. I have had the opportunity to work with amazing people and extraordinary organizations. Is it a halcyon existence? No, I don't have the stability and comfort I enjoyed as an employee in a secure public sector job, but the rewards and personal development opportunities are amazing.

Now I'm here, swimming with the dolphins, I couldn't go back.

Transmit

● Never stop exploring, challenging, hypothesizing, experimenting and learning. Remember: it is those people who are open-ended and curious who love and lead change best.

Change

# SOURCES

Books and articles

Arntz, Arnoud and Hopmans, Miranda, 'Under-predicted Pain Disrupts More than Correctly Predicted Pain, but Does not Hurt More', *Behaviour Research and Therapy* 36(12) (Dec. 1998), 1121–9

Barbe, W. B. and Swassing, R. H., *Teaching Through Modality Strengths: Concepts and Practice*, Zaner-Bloser, 1979

Bass, Bernard M., *From Transactional to Transformational Leadership: Learning to Share the Vision*, Elsevier, 1990

Carnegie, Dale, *How to Win Friends and Influence People*, Simon and Schuster, 1936

Cope, Andy and Whittaker, Andy, *The Art of Being Brilliant*, Balloon View, 2010

Covey, Steven, *The Seven Habits of Highly Effective People*, 15th anniversary edn, Simon & Schuster, 2004

Gilbreth, Frank B., *Motion Study: A Method for Increasing the Efficiency of the Workman*, Van Nostrand, 1910

Hallowell, Edward M., *Crazy Busy: Overstretched, Overbooked, and About to Snap! Strategies for Handling Your Fast-Paced Life*, Ballantine, 2007

Handy, Charles, *The Hungry Spirit*, Broadway, 1999

Jeffers, Susan, *Feel the Fear and Do It Anyway*, Century, 1987

Kennedy, Robert F., *RFK: Collected Speeches*, Viking Adult, 1993

Latham, G. and Locke, Edwin A., 'Building a Practically Useful Theory of Goal Setting and Task Motivation', *American Psychologist* 57(9) (2002), 705–17

Lerner, Clare and Dombro, Amy Laura, *Bringing Up Baby: Three Steps to Making Good Decisions in Your Child's First Years*, Zero to Three, 2004

Molloy, Donna, White, Clarissa and Hosfield, Nicola, *Understanding Youth Participation in Local Government: A Qualitative Study*, DTLR, 2002

Prochaska, J. O. and DiClemente, C. C., 'The Transtheoretical Approach', in: J. C. Norcross and M. R. Goldfried (eds.), *Handbook of Psychotherapy Integration*, 2nd edn, Oxford University Press, 2005, pp. 147–71

Robinson, Sir Ken, *The Element: How Finding Your Passion Changes Everything*, Viking Penguin, 2009

Robinson, Sir Ken, *Out of Our Minds*, Capstone, 2011

Scaglione, Robert and Cummins, William, *Karate of Okinawa: Building Warrior Spirit*, Tuttle Publishing, 1993

Schwartz, Barry, *The Paradox of Choice: Why More Is Less*, Ecco, 2004

Taylor, Frederick Winslow, *The Principles of Scientific Management*, Harper & Brothers, 1911

Wallison, Peter, *Ronald Reagan: The Power of Conviction and the Success of His Presidency*, Basic Books, 2002

Wildschut, Tim, Sedikides, Constantine, Arndt, Jamie and Routledge, Clay, 'Nostalgia: Content, Triggers, Functions', *Journal of Personality and Social Psychology* 91(5) (Nov. 2006), 975–93

Young, William P., *The Shack*, Windblown Media, 2007

## Internet resources

ABA, The American Branding Association: http://seattlebranding.org/

Association for Psychological Science: www.psychologicalscience.org/

Blue Man Group: www.blueman.com

Bossart, Donald E., 'Growing Through Conflict': www.religion-online.org/showarticle.asp?title=297

Brown, Stuart: National Institute for Play: http://nifplay.org

Brown, Stuart: 2009 TED speech: www.ted.com/talks/view/lang/en//id/483

Canadian Mental Health Association: www.cmha.ca/

Conscious Capitalism: http://consciouscapitalism.org/

Fox, Matthew: www.matthewfox.org/

Global Entrepreneurship and Development Institute: www.thegedi.org

House of Commons Research Papers: www.ukpolitical.info/Turnout45.htm

Jenkins, Henry, Purushotma, R., Weigel, M., Clinton, K. and Robison, A. J., 'Confronting the Challenges of Participatory Culture: Media Education for the 21st Century', retrieved from www.mitpress.mit.edu/books/chapters/Confronting_the_Challenges.pdf

kaizen: http://uk.kaizen.com

Land, Edwin H., Ninth Annual Arthur Dehon Little Memorial Lecture, Massachusetts Institute of Technology, 22 May 1957: http://groups.csail.mit.edu/mac/users/hal/misc/generation-of-greatness.html

Lickerman, Alex: www.psychologytoday.com/experts/alex-lickerman-md

Robbins, Anthony: www.anthony-robbins.org.uk/

Stepanek, Mattie J. T.: www.mattieonline.com/

Sybervision, 'The World's Hundred Greatest People': www.sybervision.com/People

Tracy, Brian: www.briantracy.com

von Oech, Roger: http://creativethink.com

Wilson, Keith A.: www.thewinningmind.com

# ACKNOWLEDGEMENTS

Writing this book has been a journey for me, a journey that has only been possible because of the people who have encouraged, supported, nagged and pushed me. I would like to take this opportunity to celebrate my rocks; those people who, in times of change, have been my constants.

Firstly my wife Lynne and my children Bethany and Andrew; without your support, patience and love, who knows where I'd be?

To my family; especially my parents, who have seen me through the best and worst of times.

To Sir Ken Robinson: my mentor, guide and inspiration.

To Brendan Barns and his team at Speakers for Business, who have made my new career happen.

To Monica Abangan and the team at The

Washington Speakers Bureau, who are helping to get my voice heard across the pond.

To Joel Rickett and his team at Portfolio Penguin, who not only understood what I wanted to say but how I should say it, as well, of course, as being prepared to print it.

To my copy-editor Trevor Horwood; so thoroughly challenging and right.

To the brilliant Richard Marston for his wonderful layout design and to Yulia Brodskaya whose cover design is truly a thing of beauty and still takes my breath away.

To Philip Dodd, whose extraordinary talent and vision as a writer and editor have transformed my words and thoughts into a book I am so proud of.

And finally, to all those people, throughout my life, who have helped me to learn to love change and to those people who have trusted me to lead them through it!

Acknowledgements